copyright © 2020 MAX DIN

All rights reserved . No part of this book may be reproduced or used in any manner without written permission of the copyright owner , except for the use of quotations and other non commercial uses permitted by copyright law .

Adult Coloring Book
Stress relieving Designs

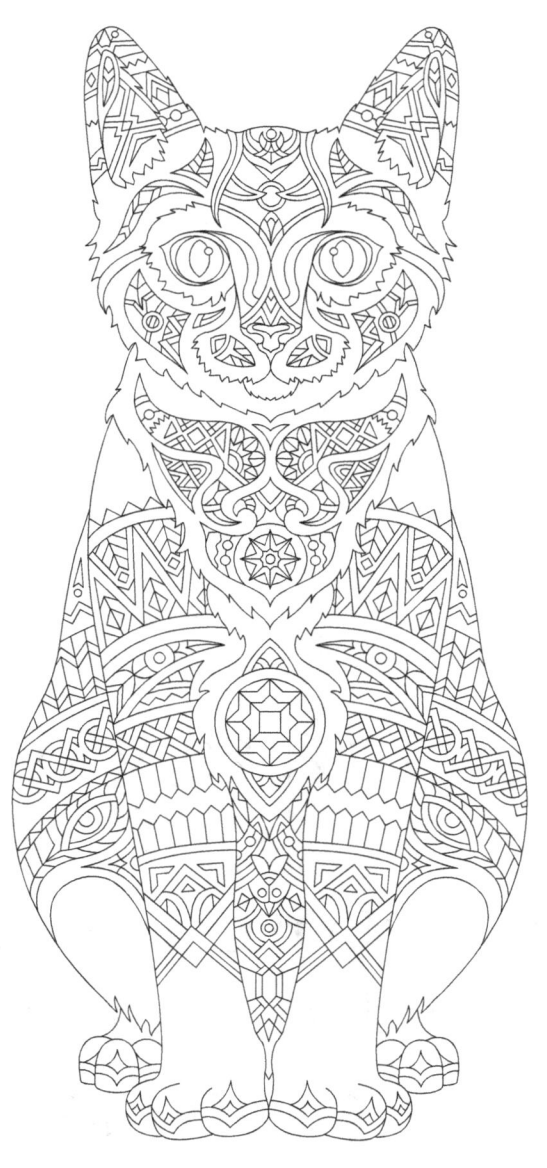

Attributed to :
freepick.com

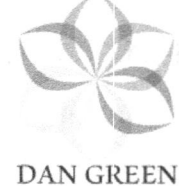

DAN GREEN

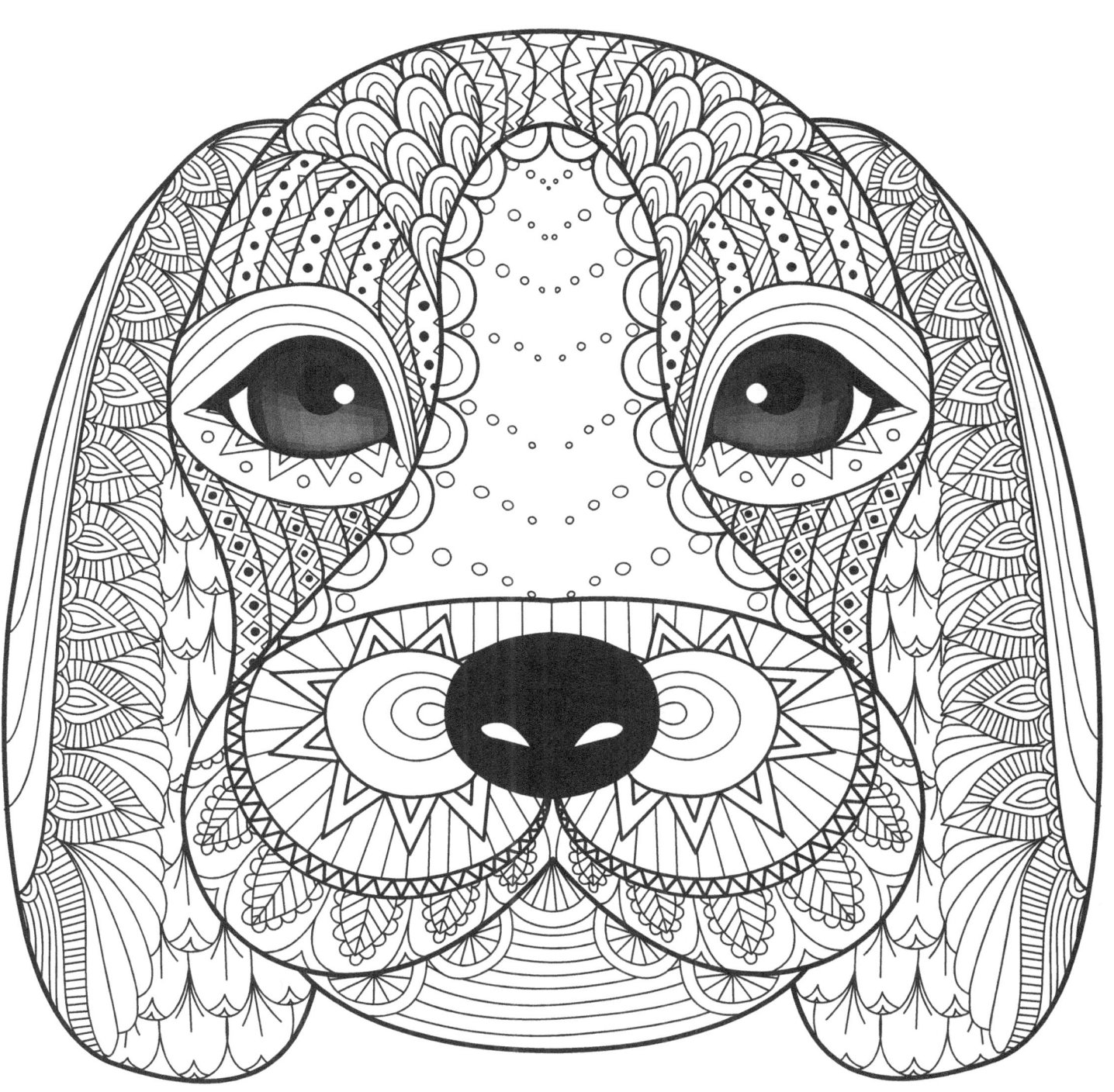

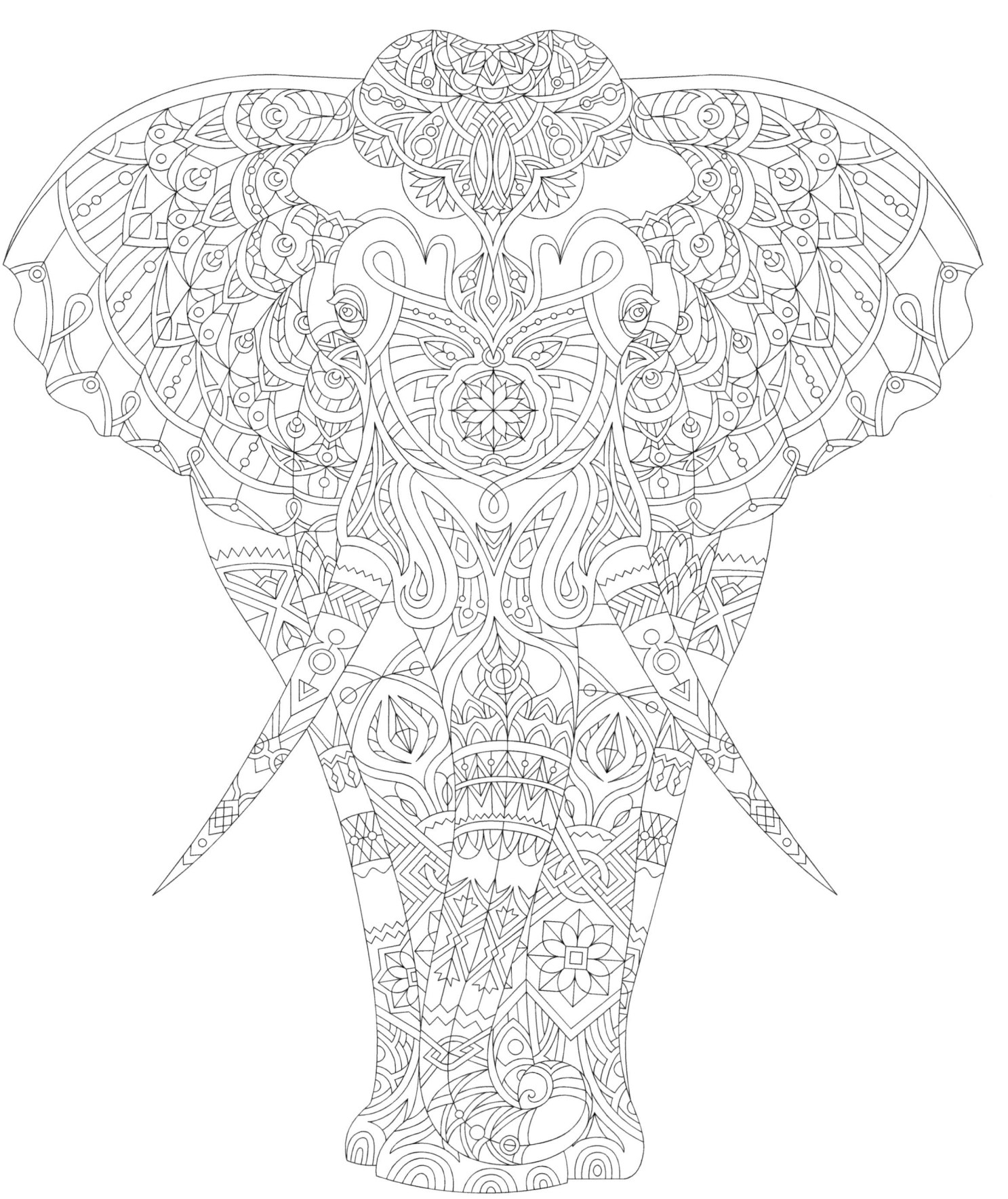

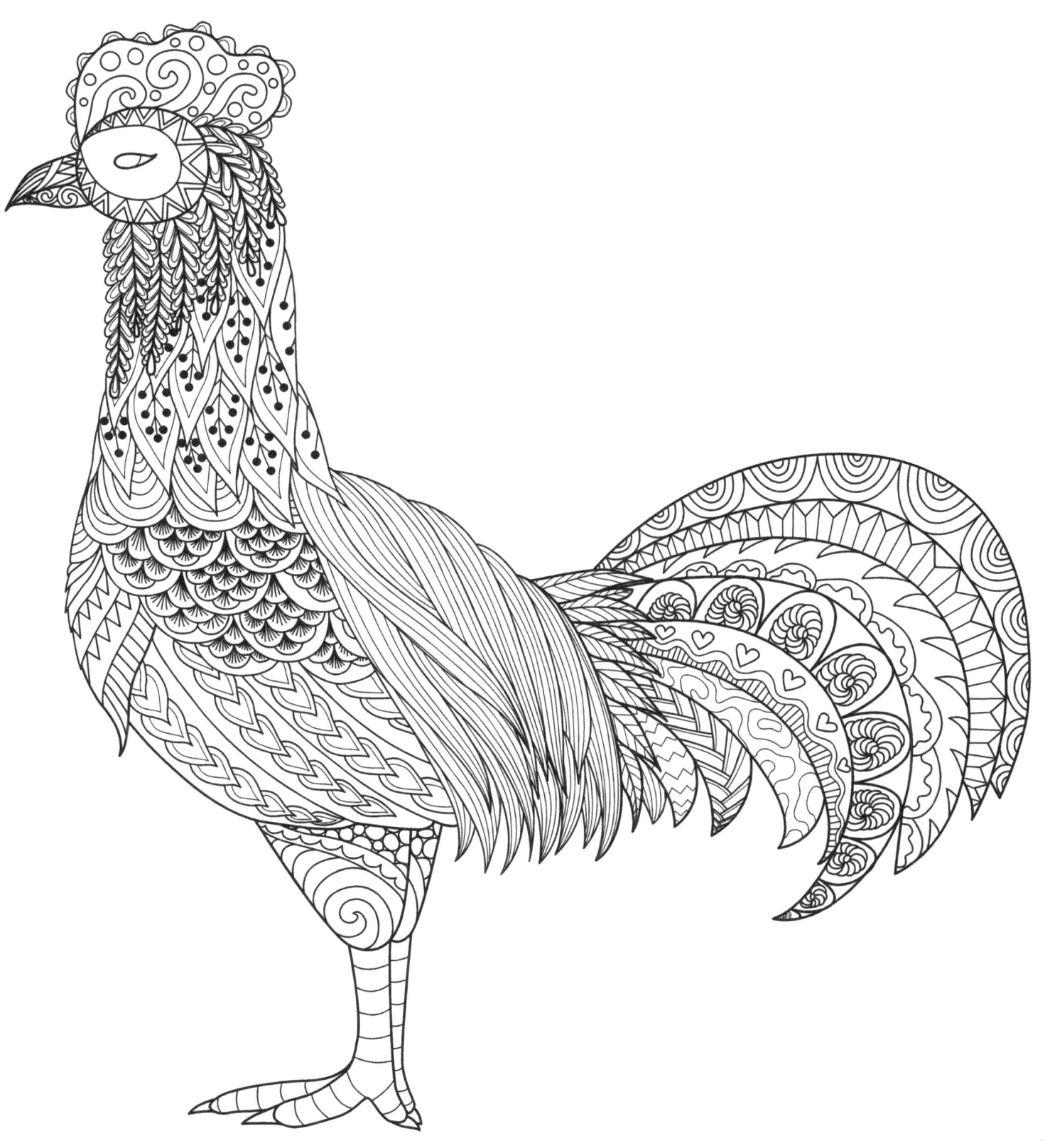

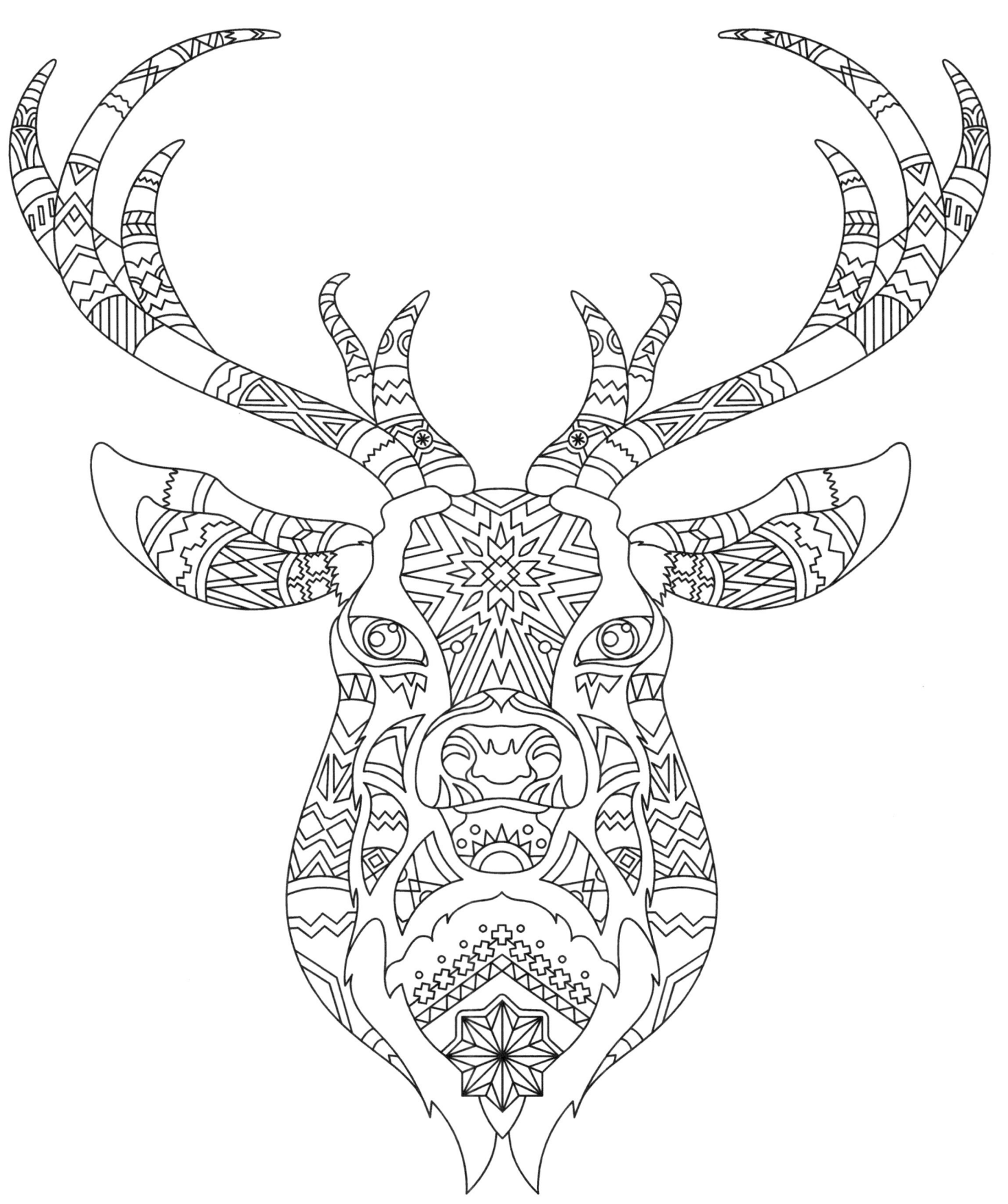

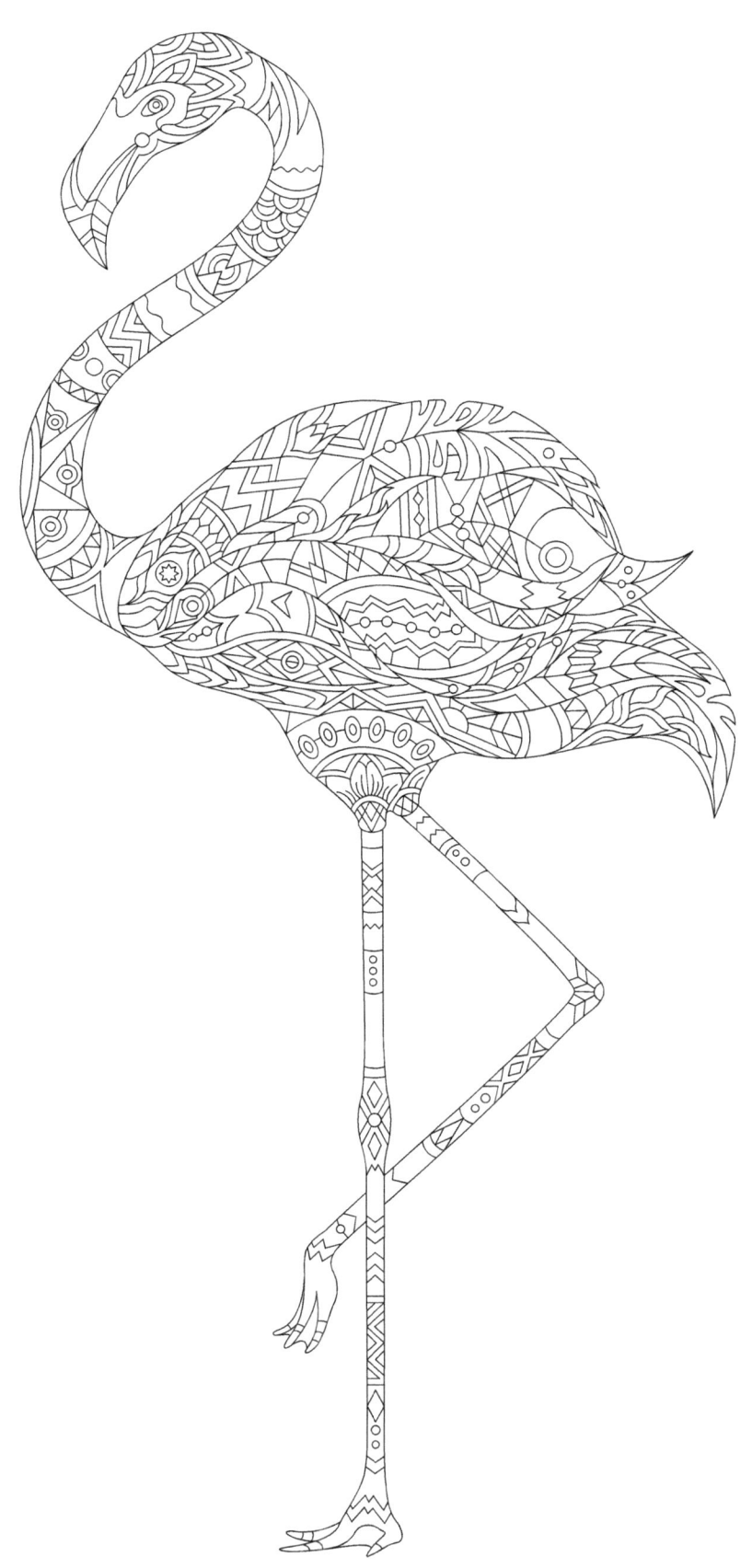

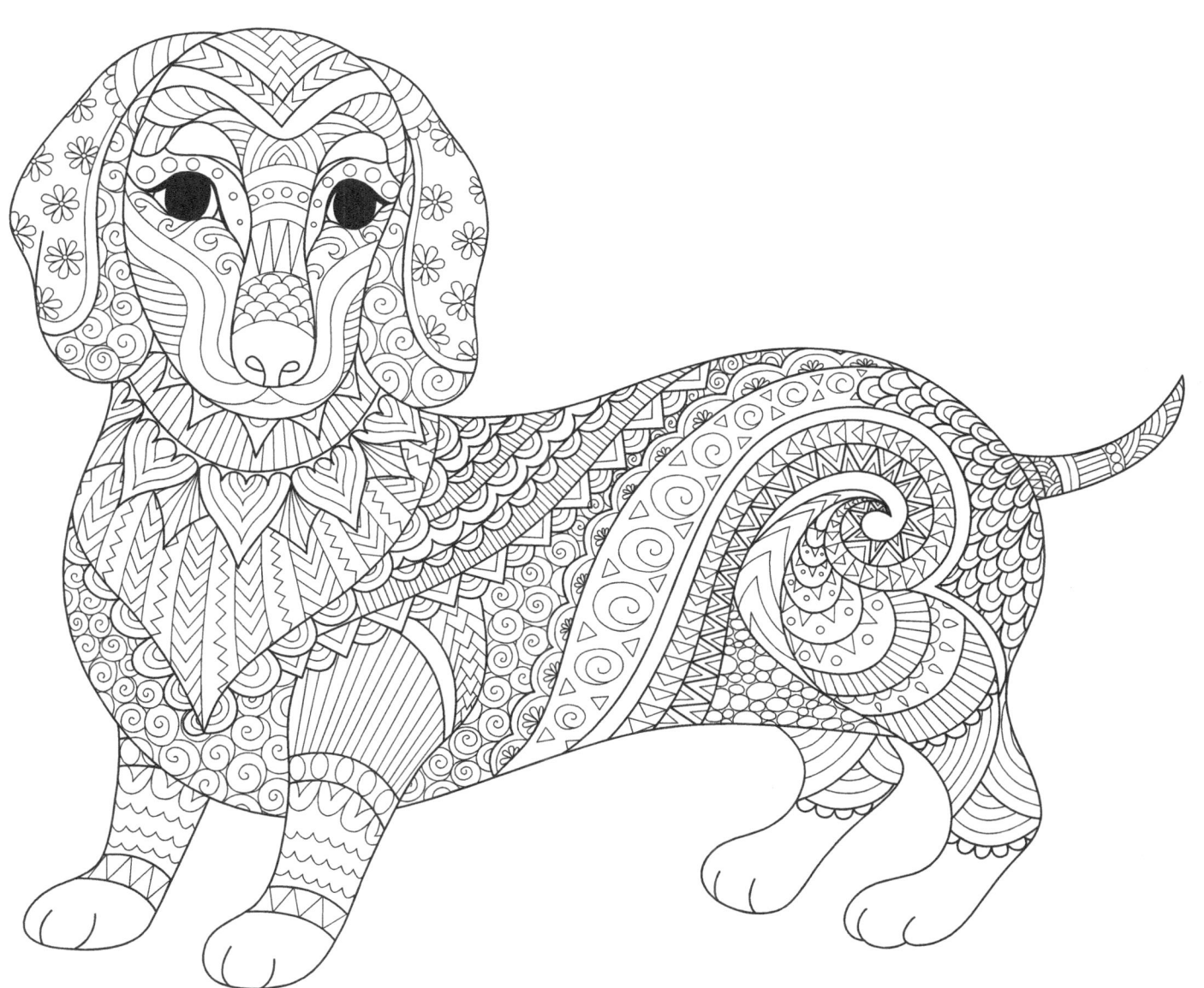

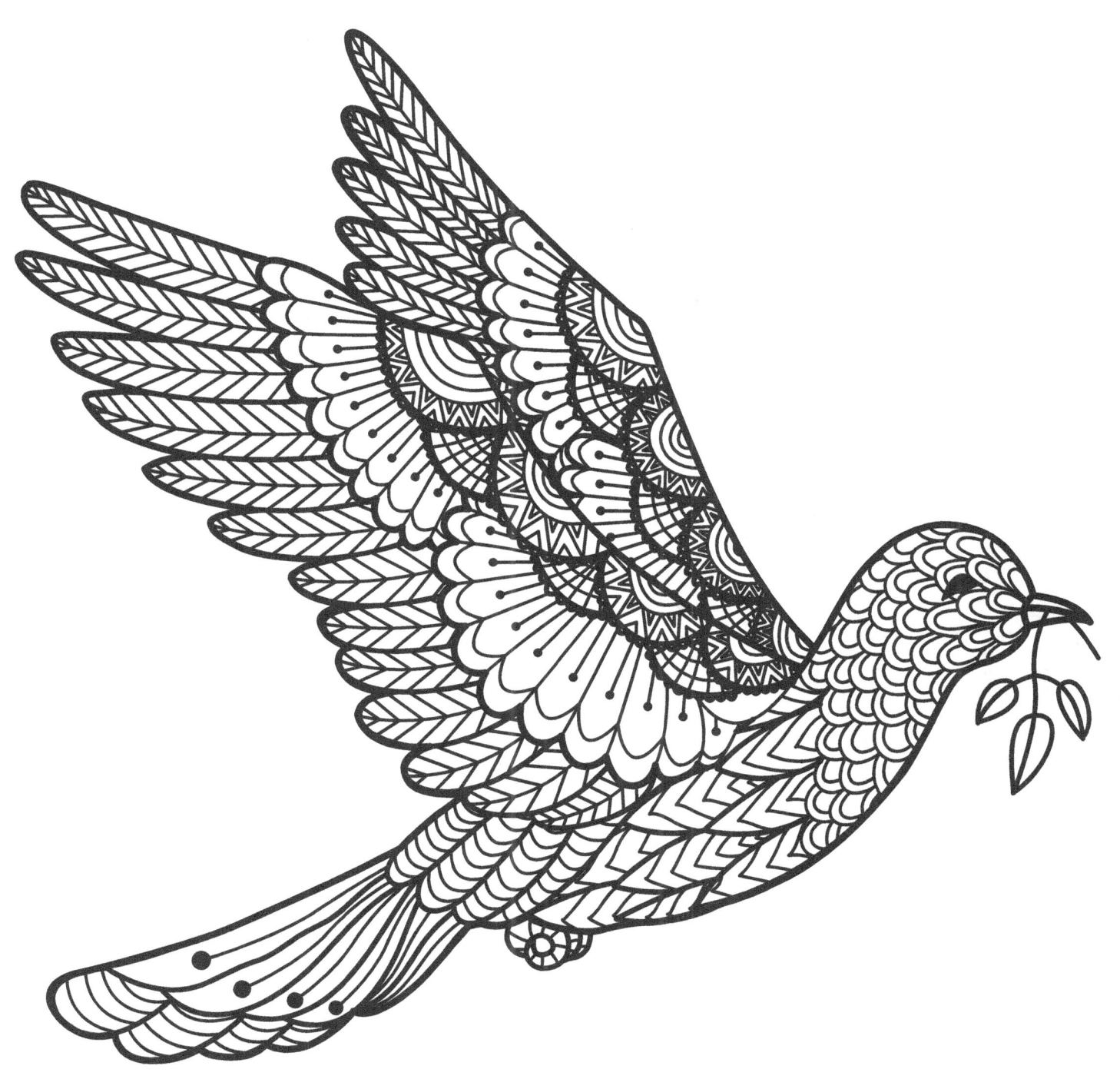

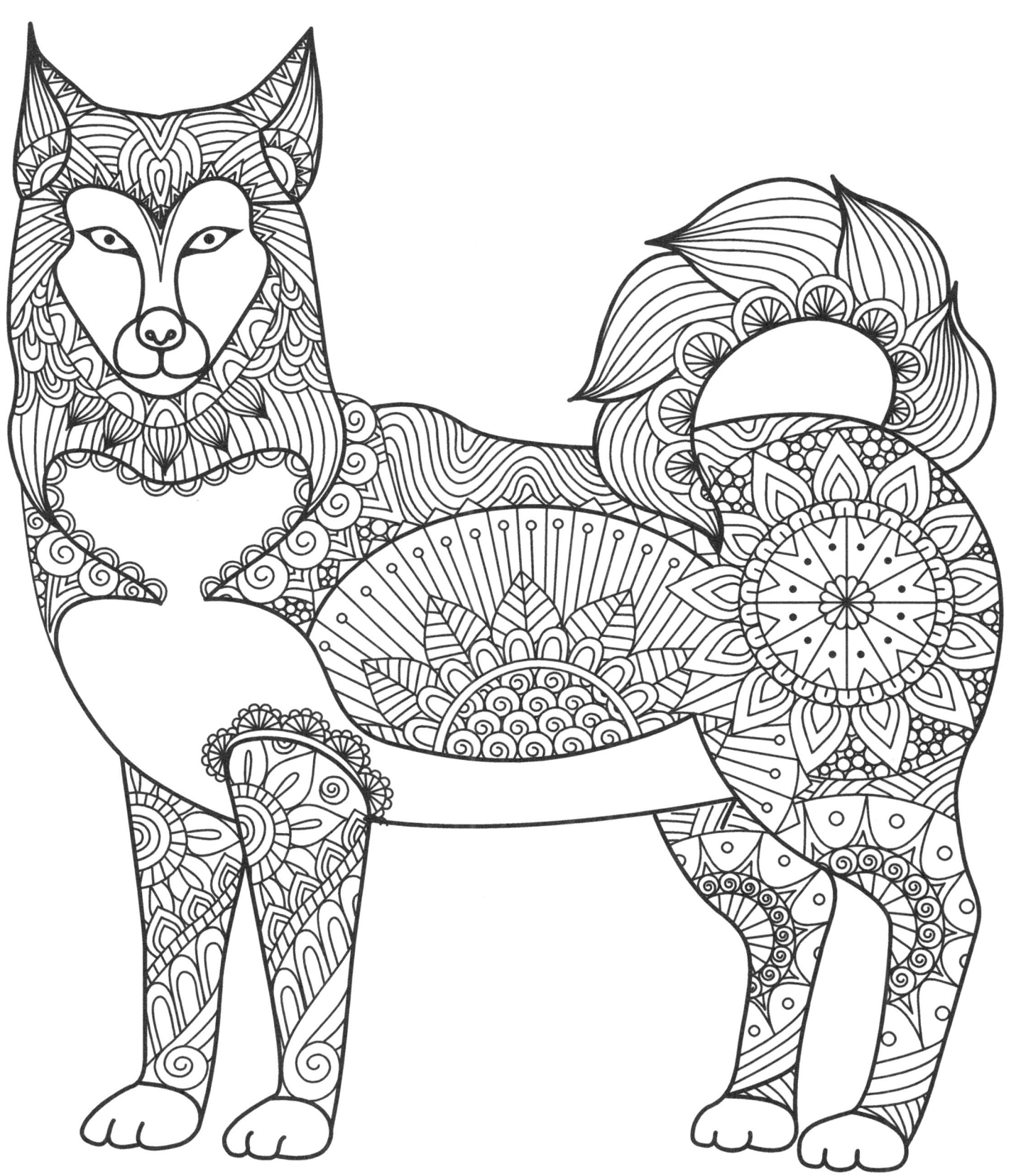

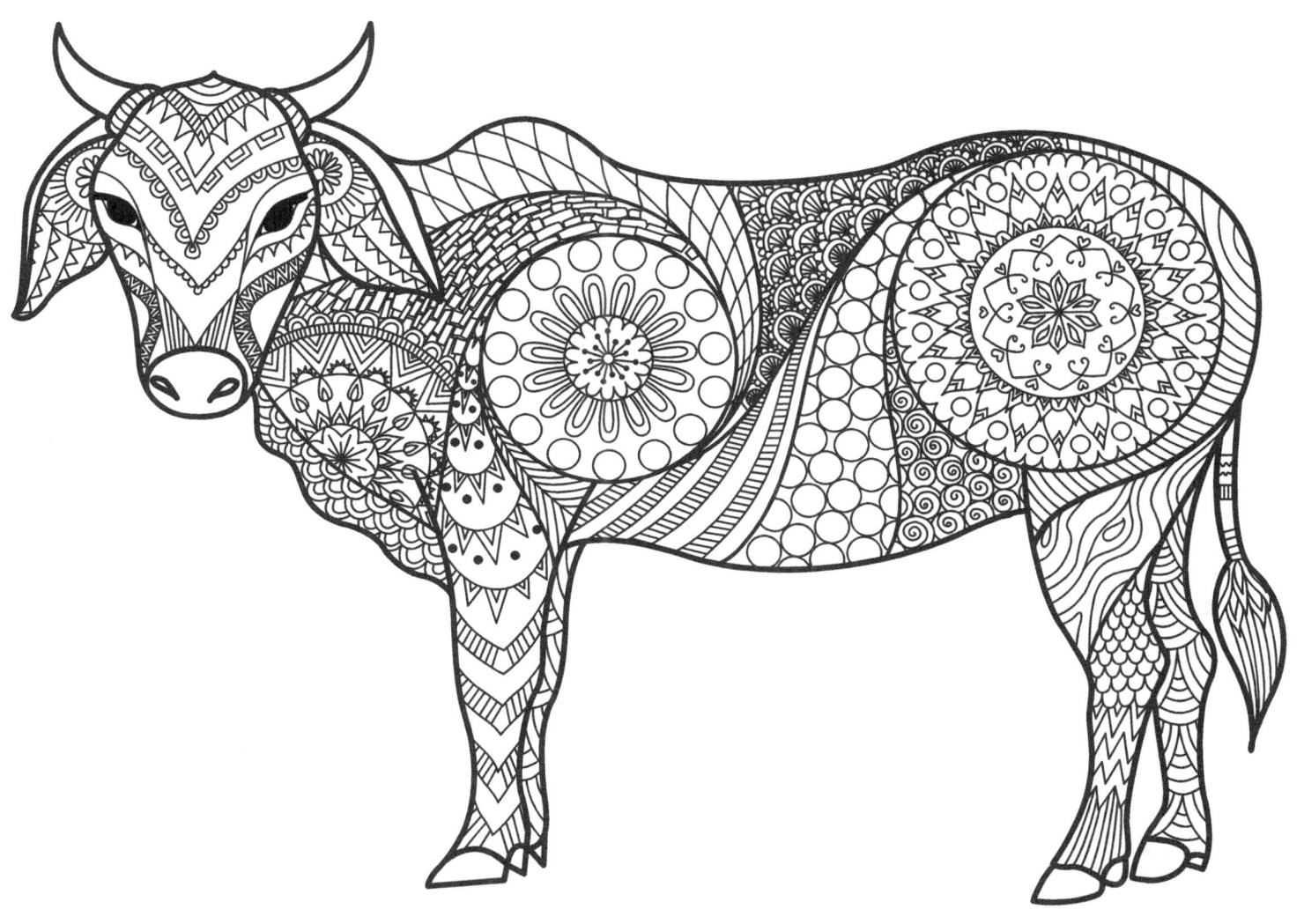

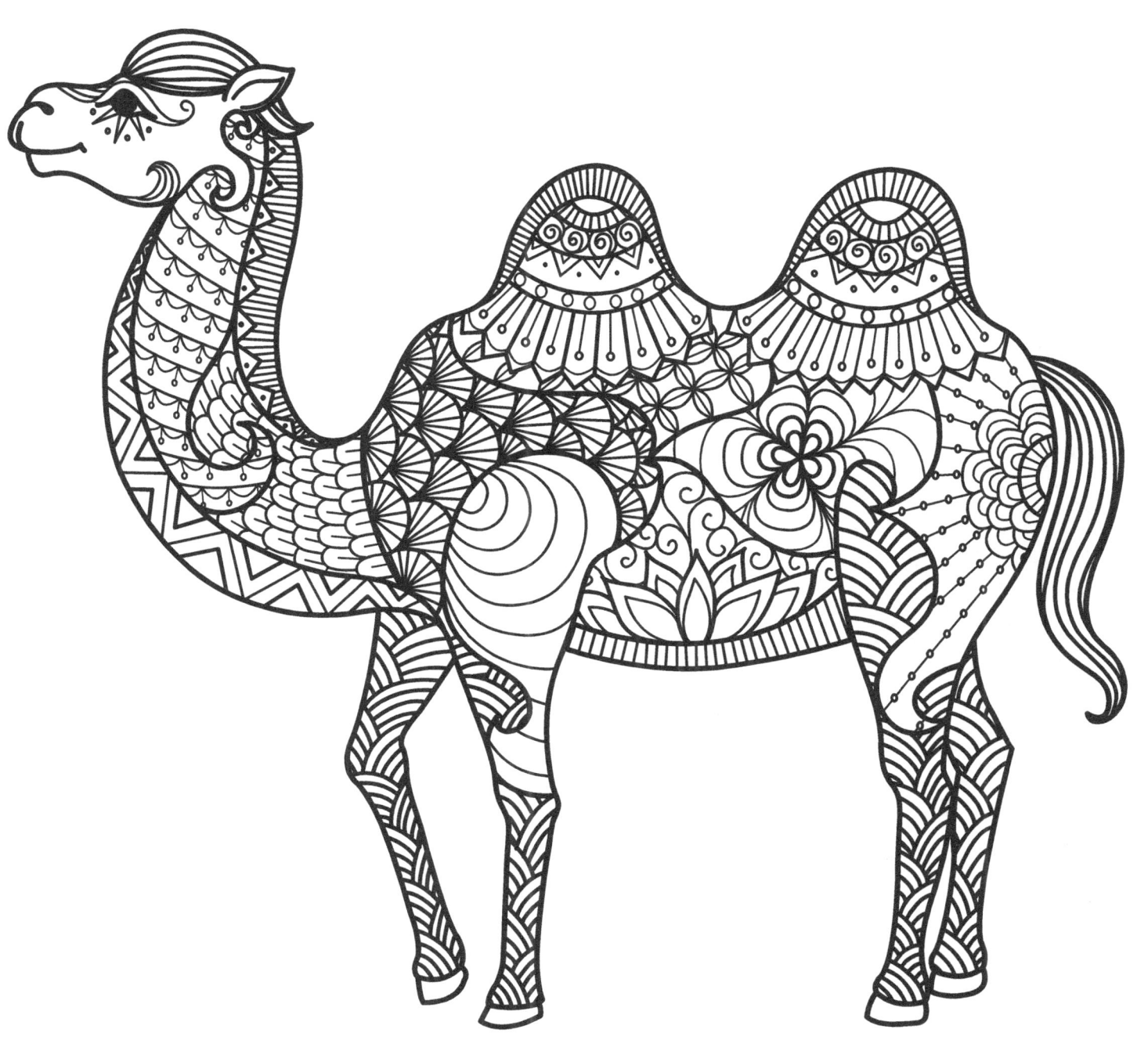

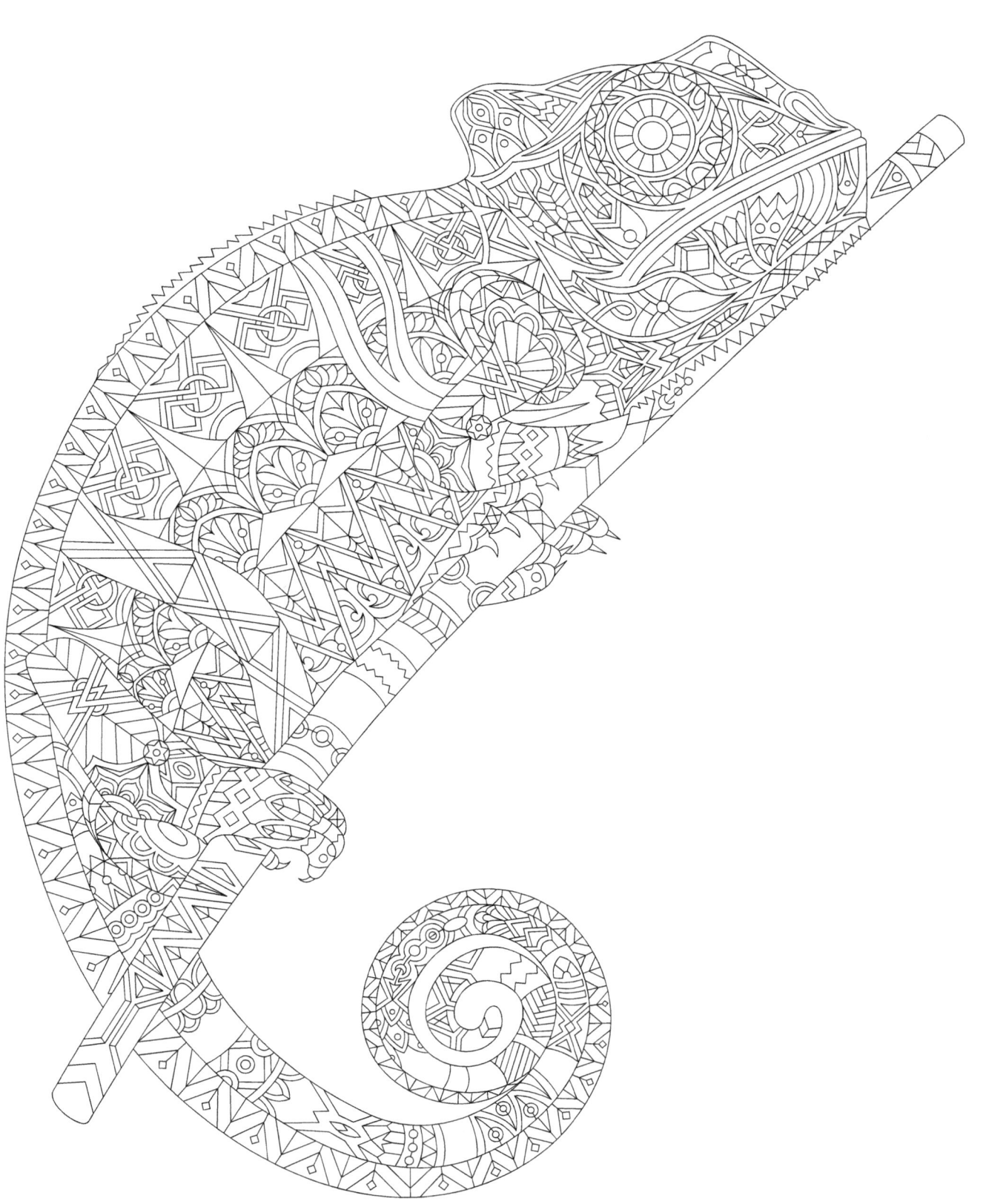

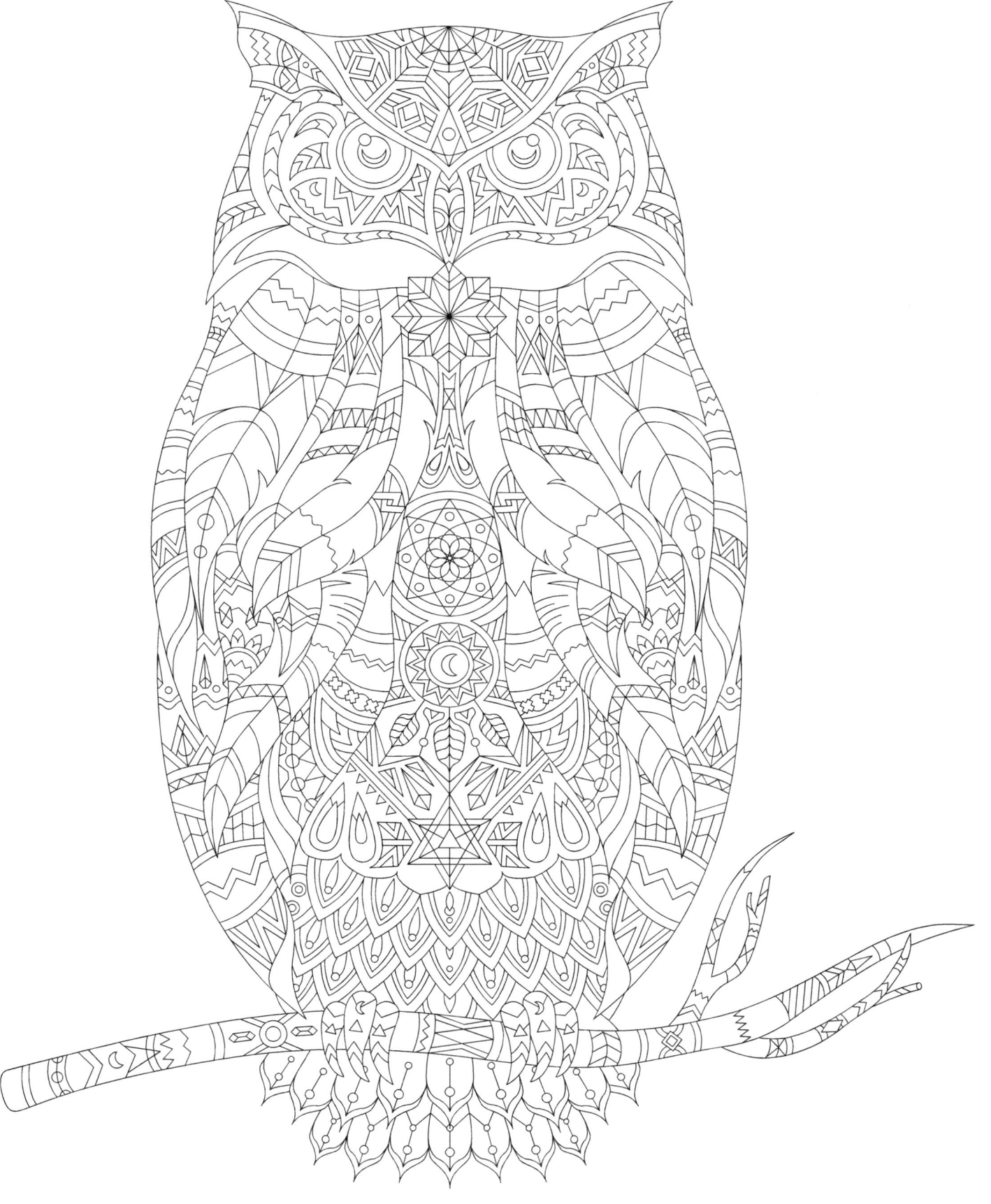

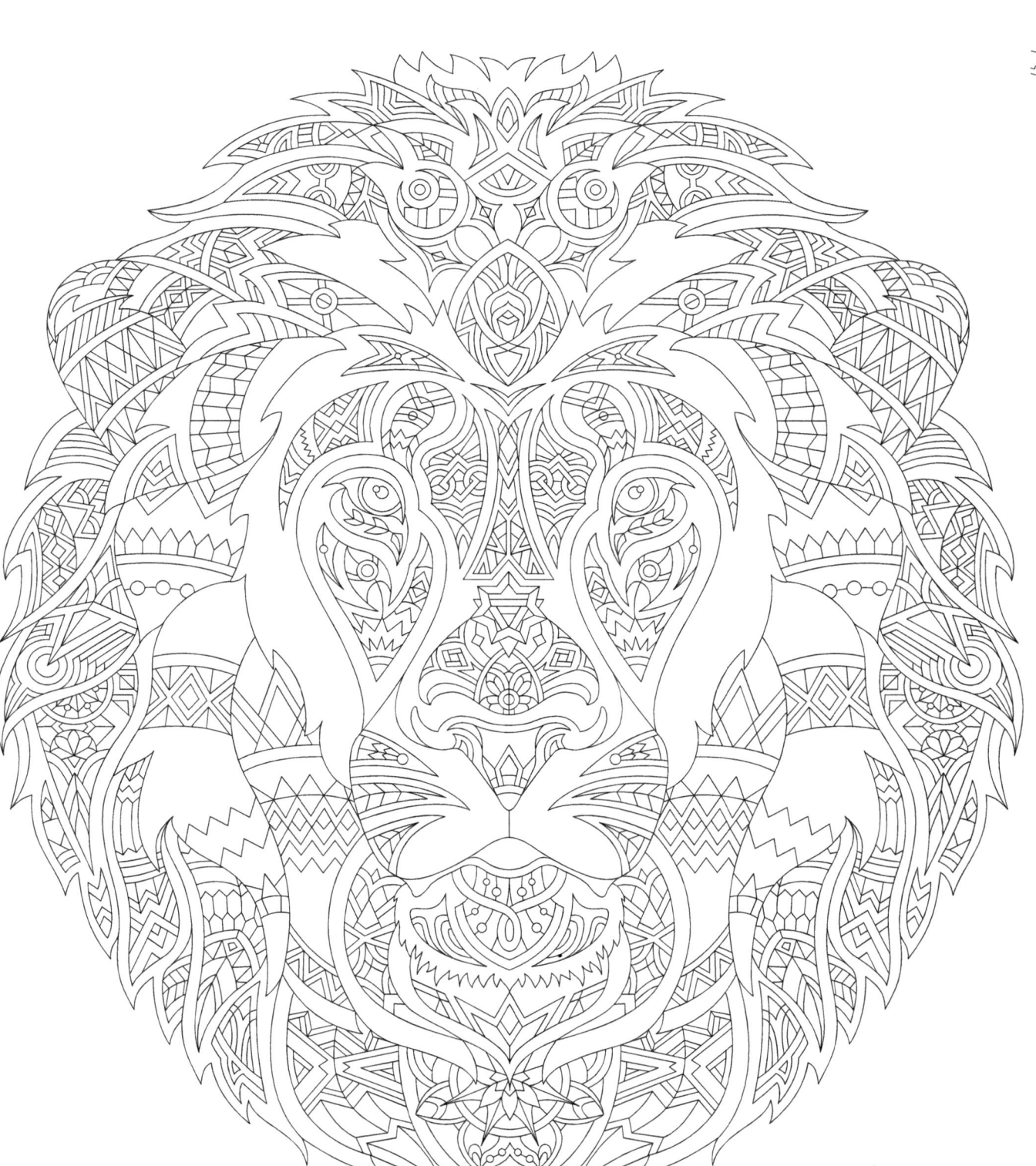

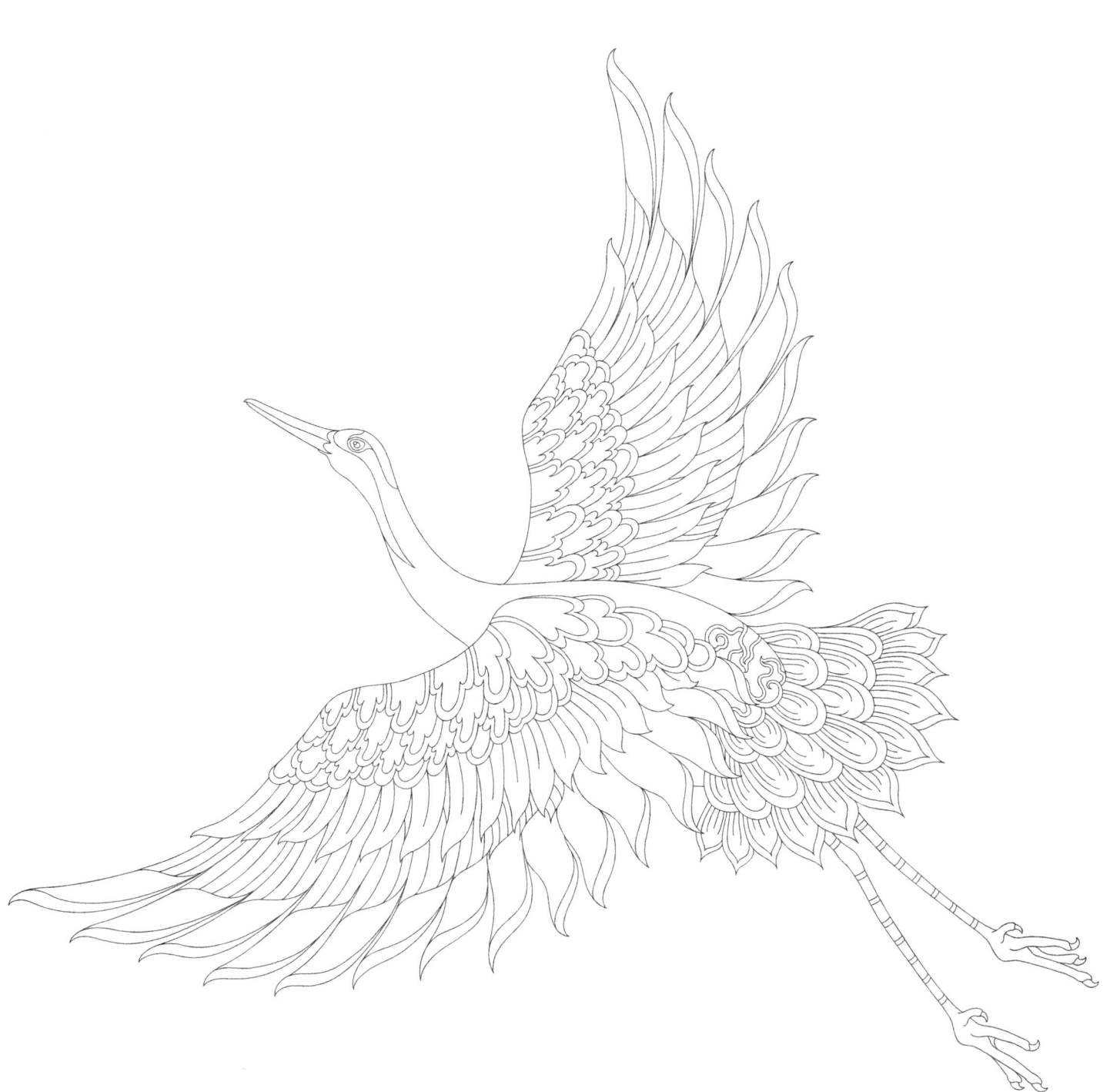

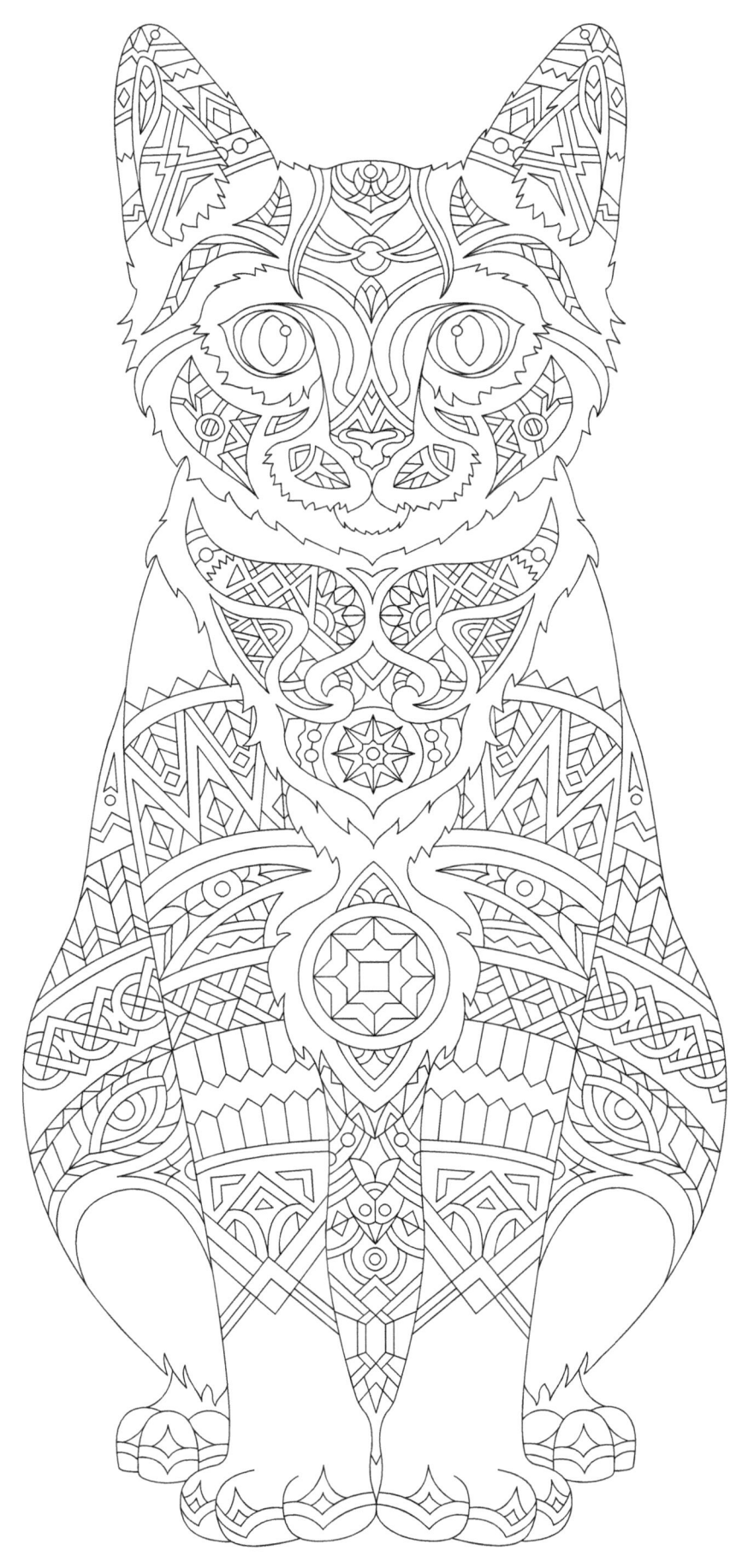

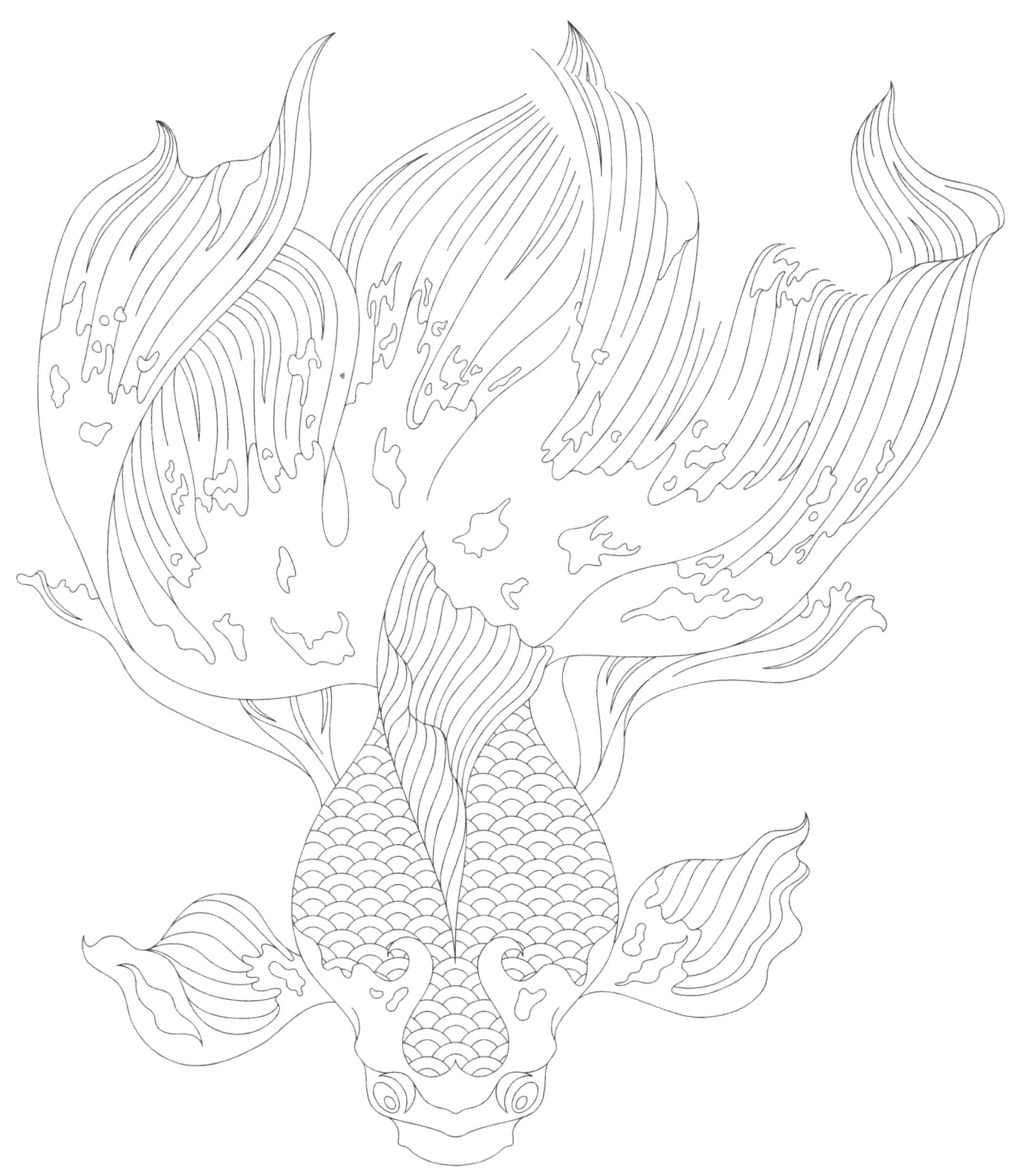

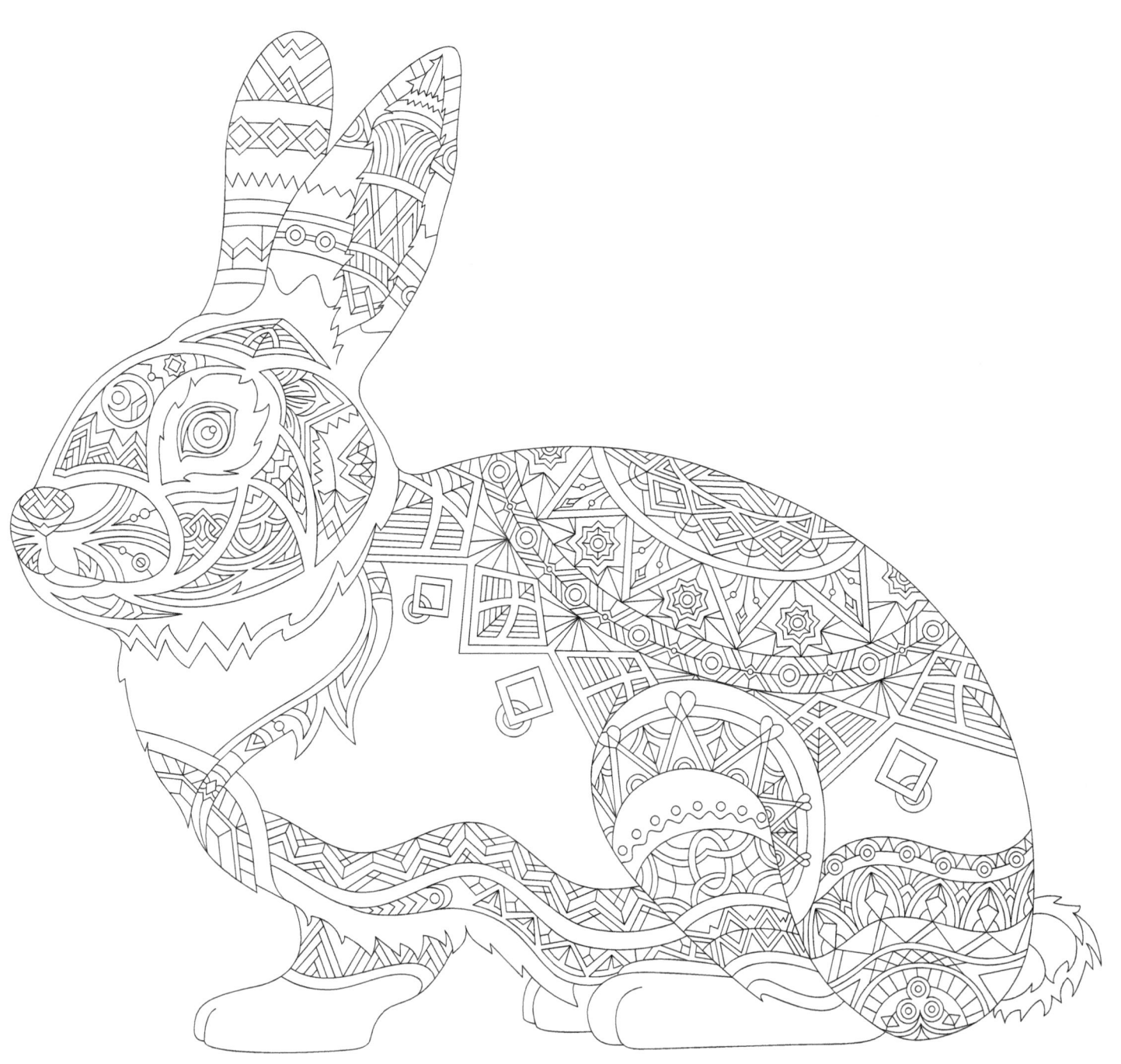

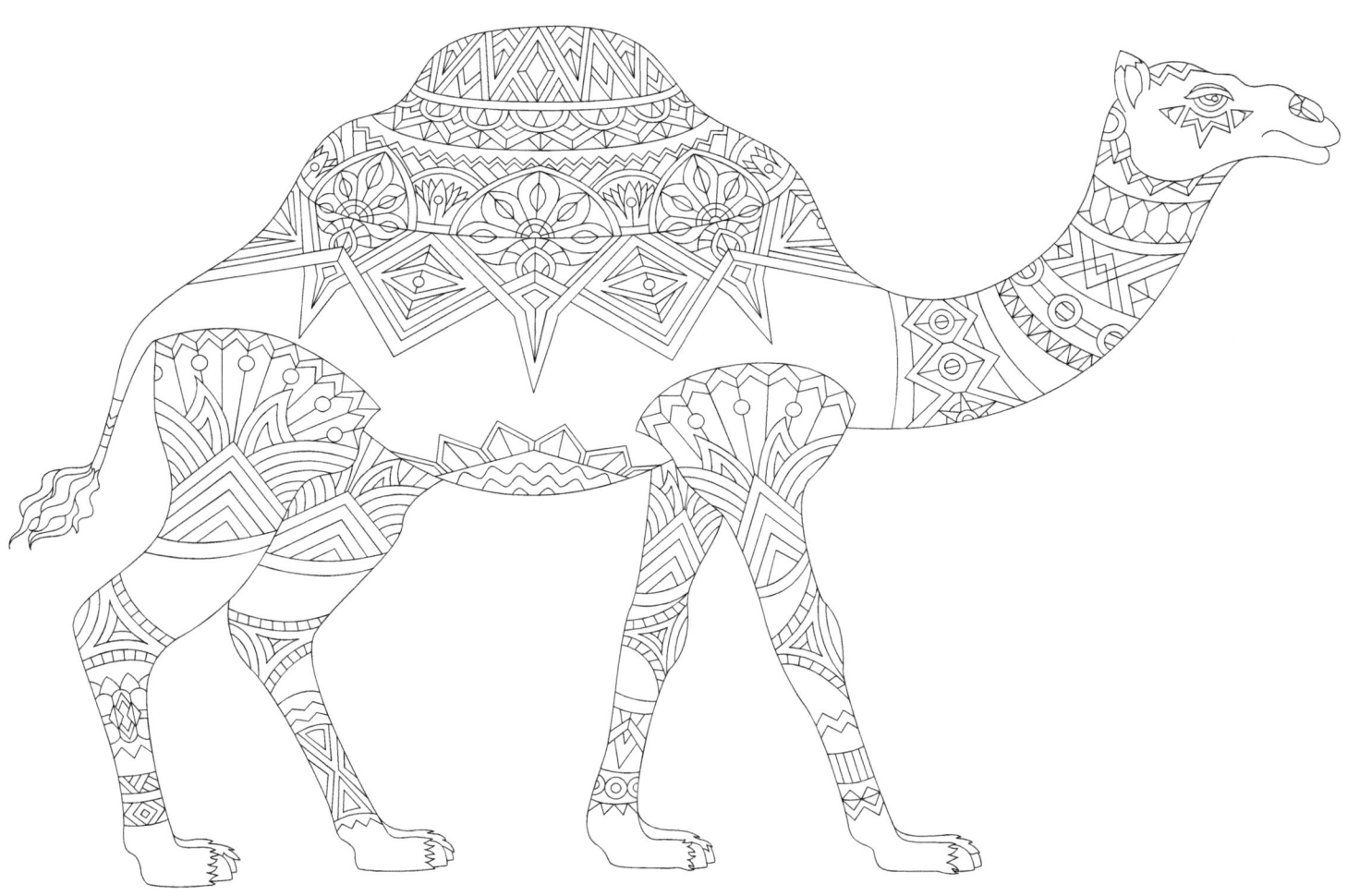

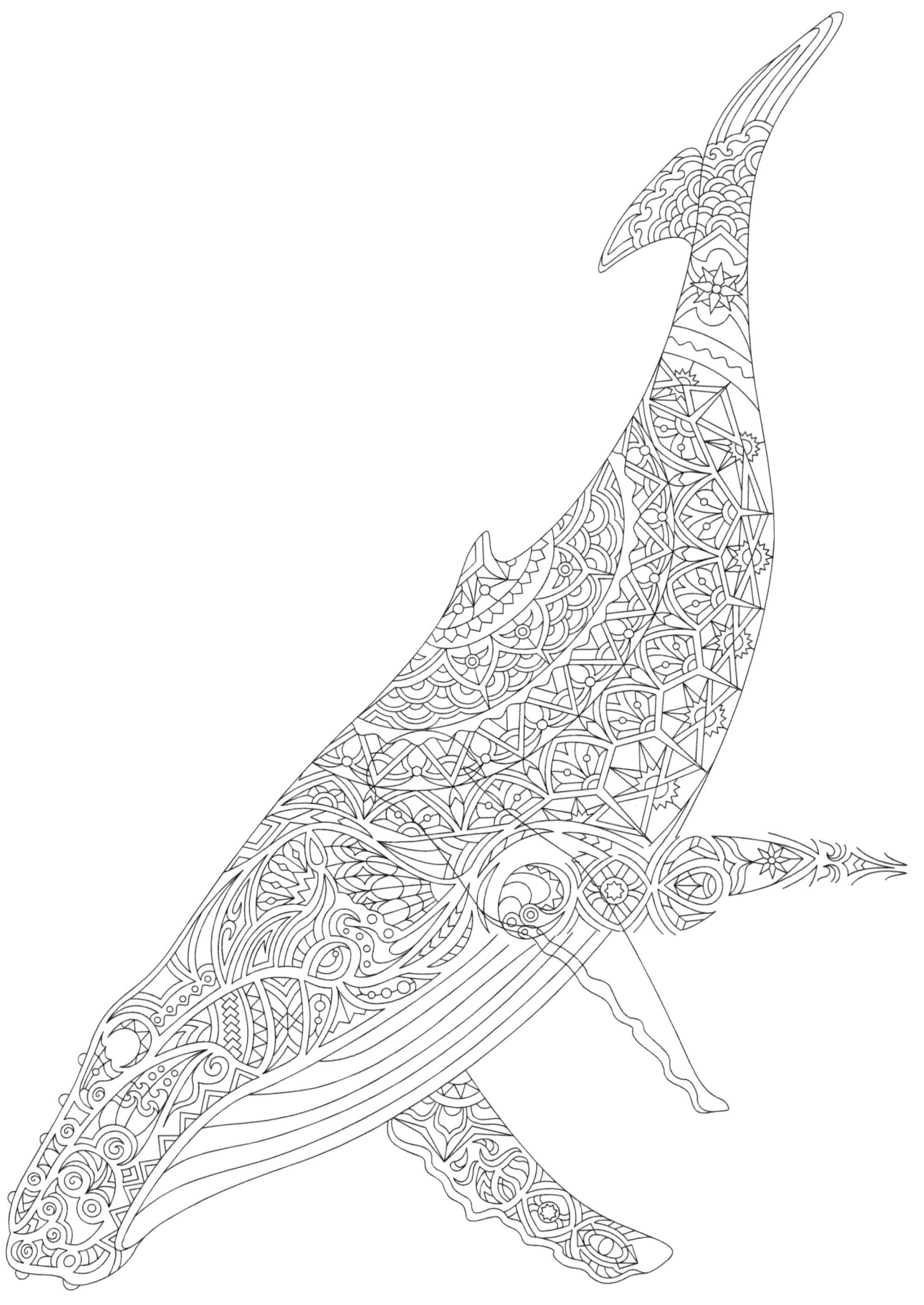

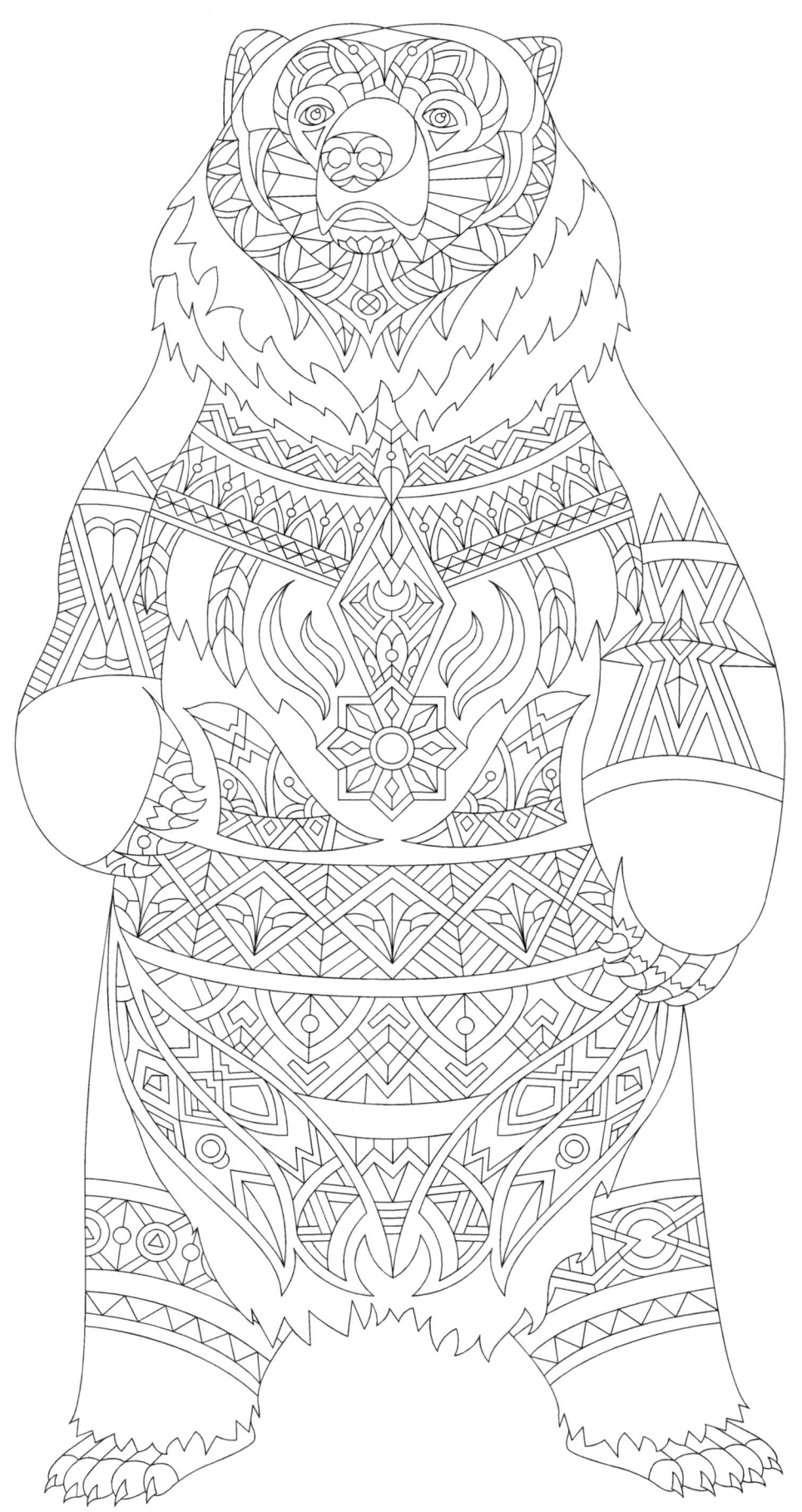

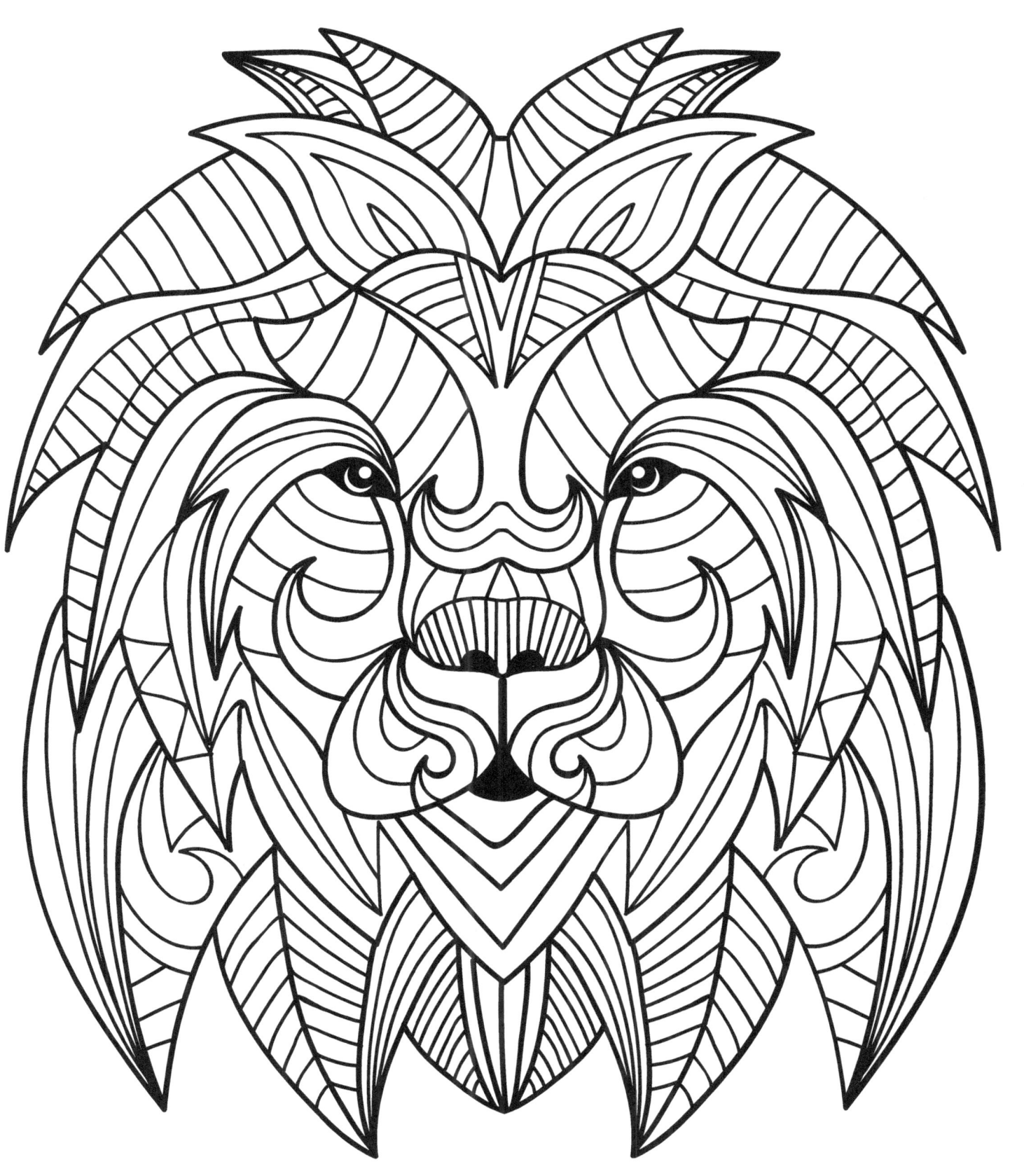

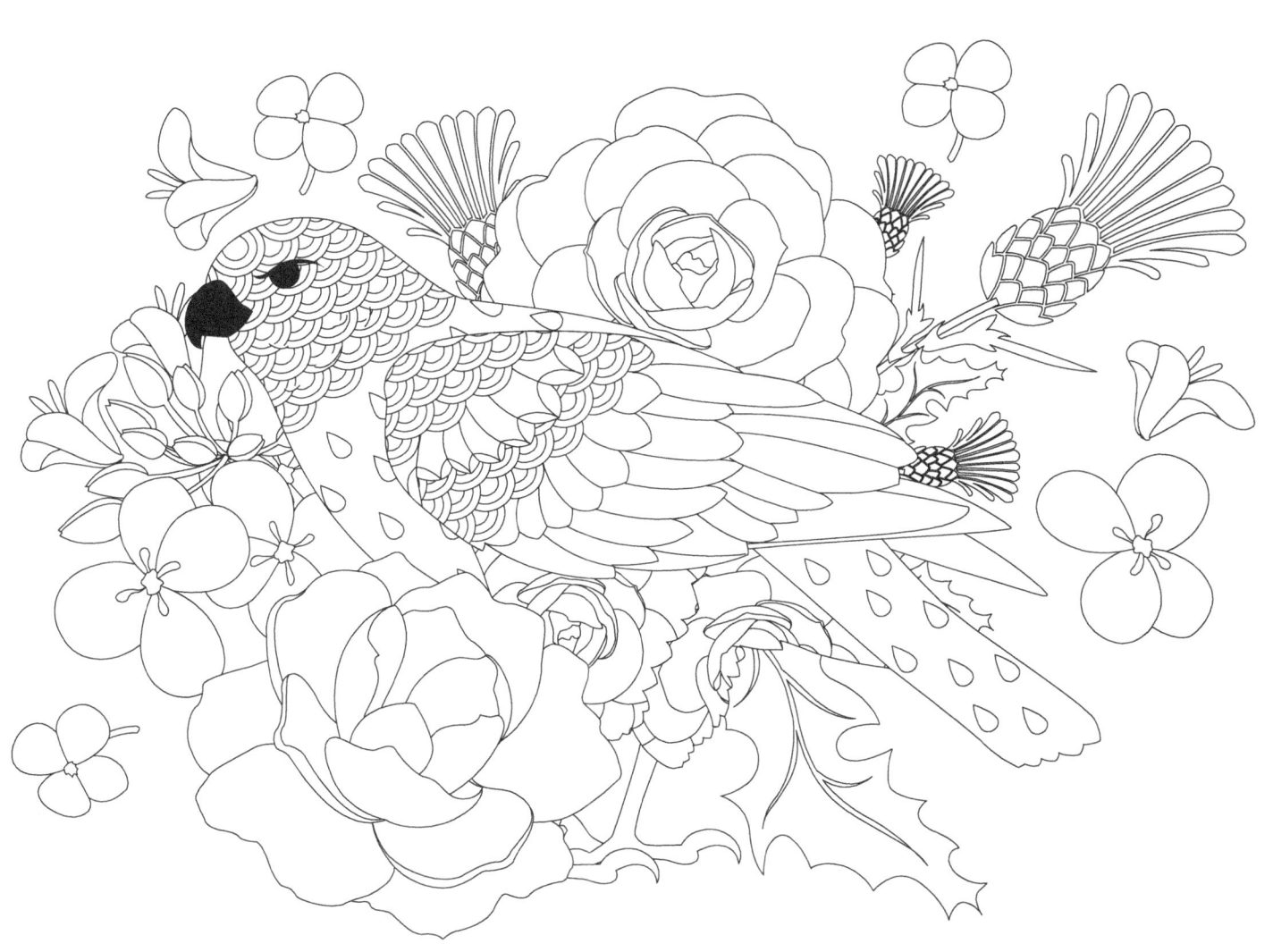

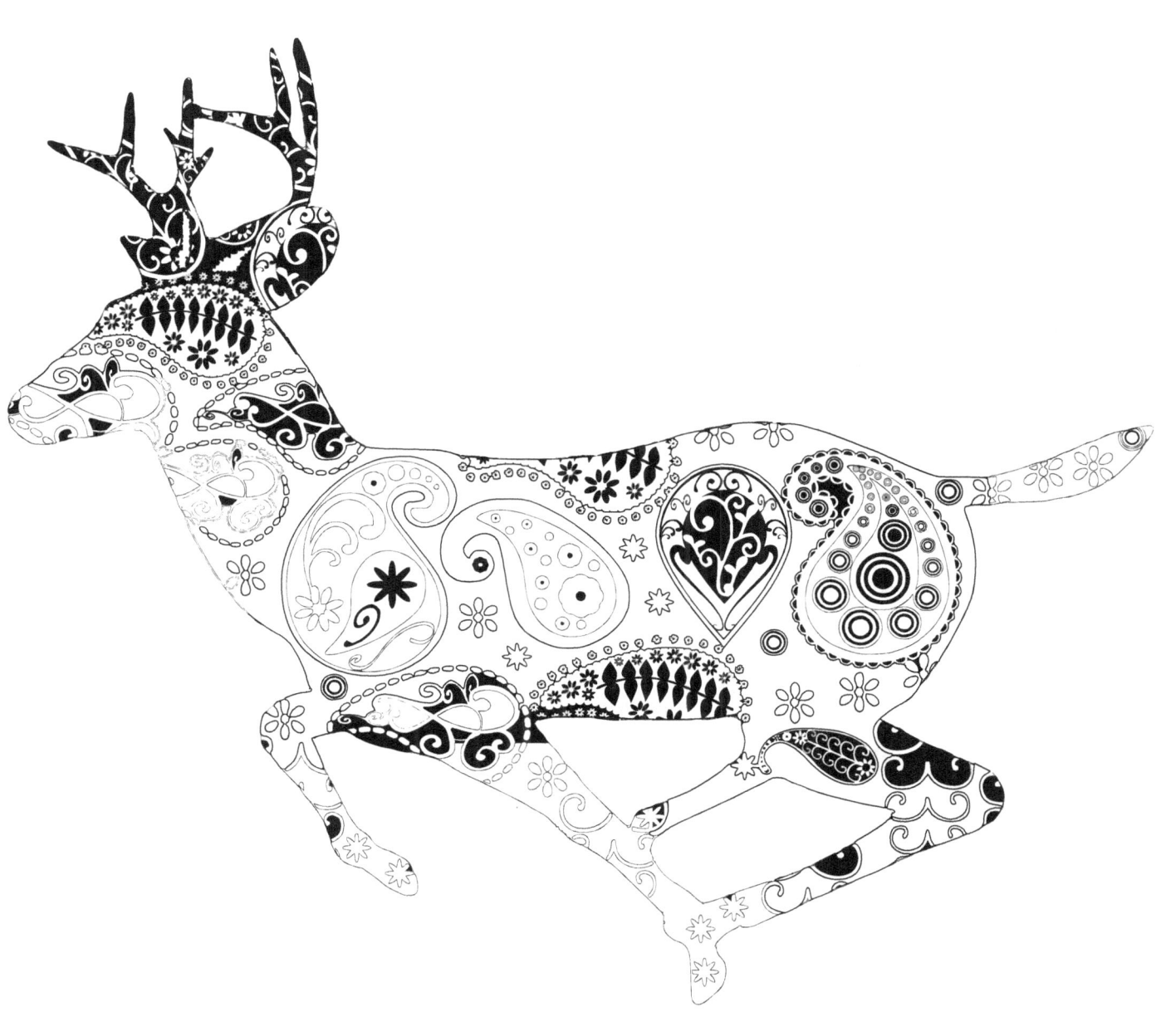

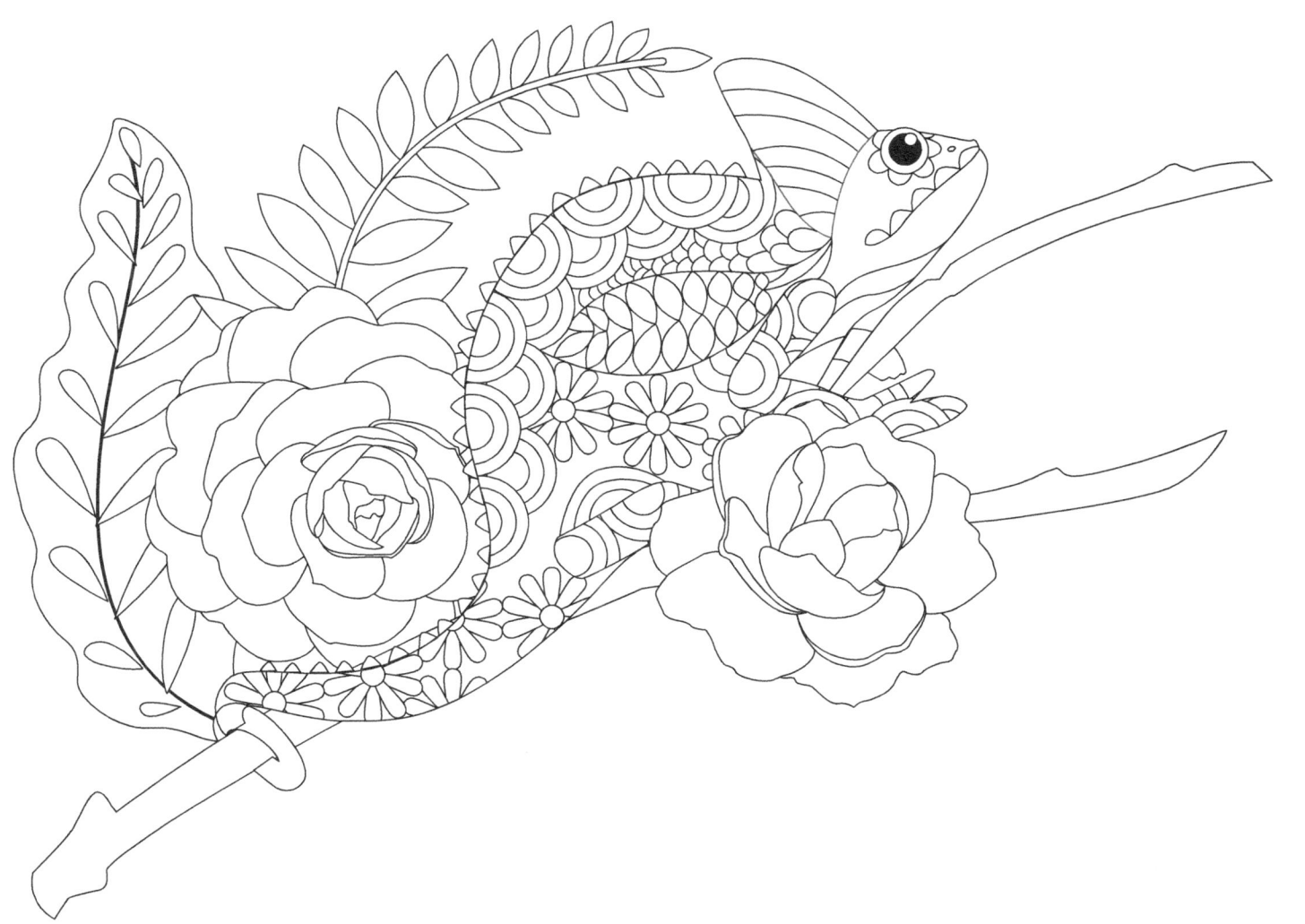

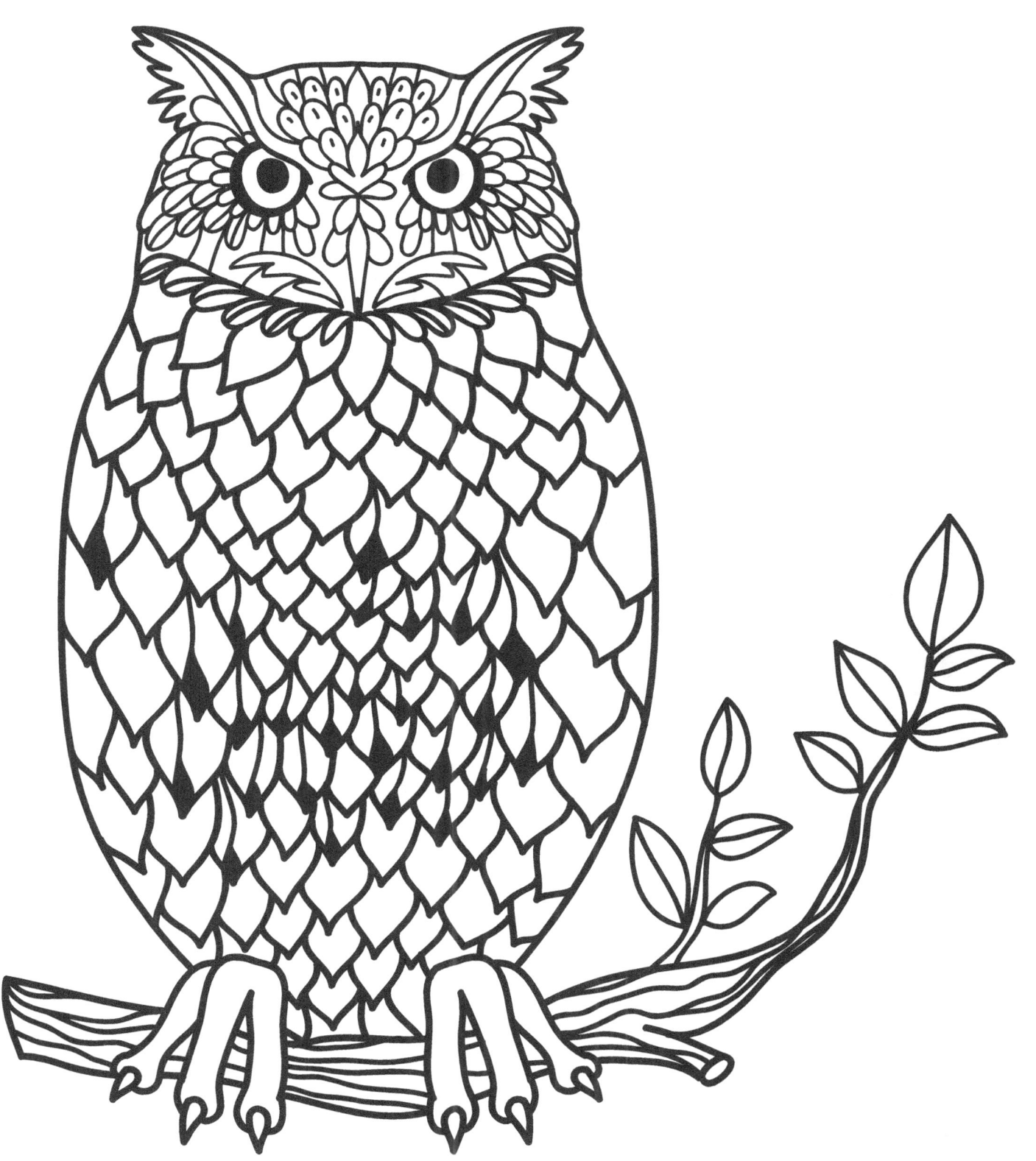

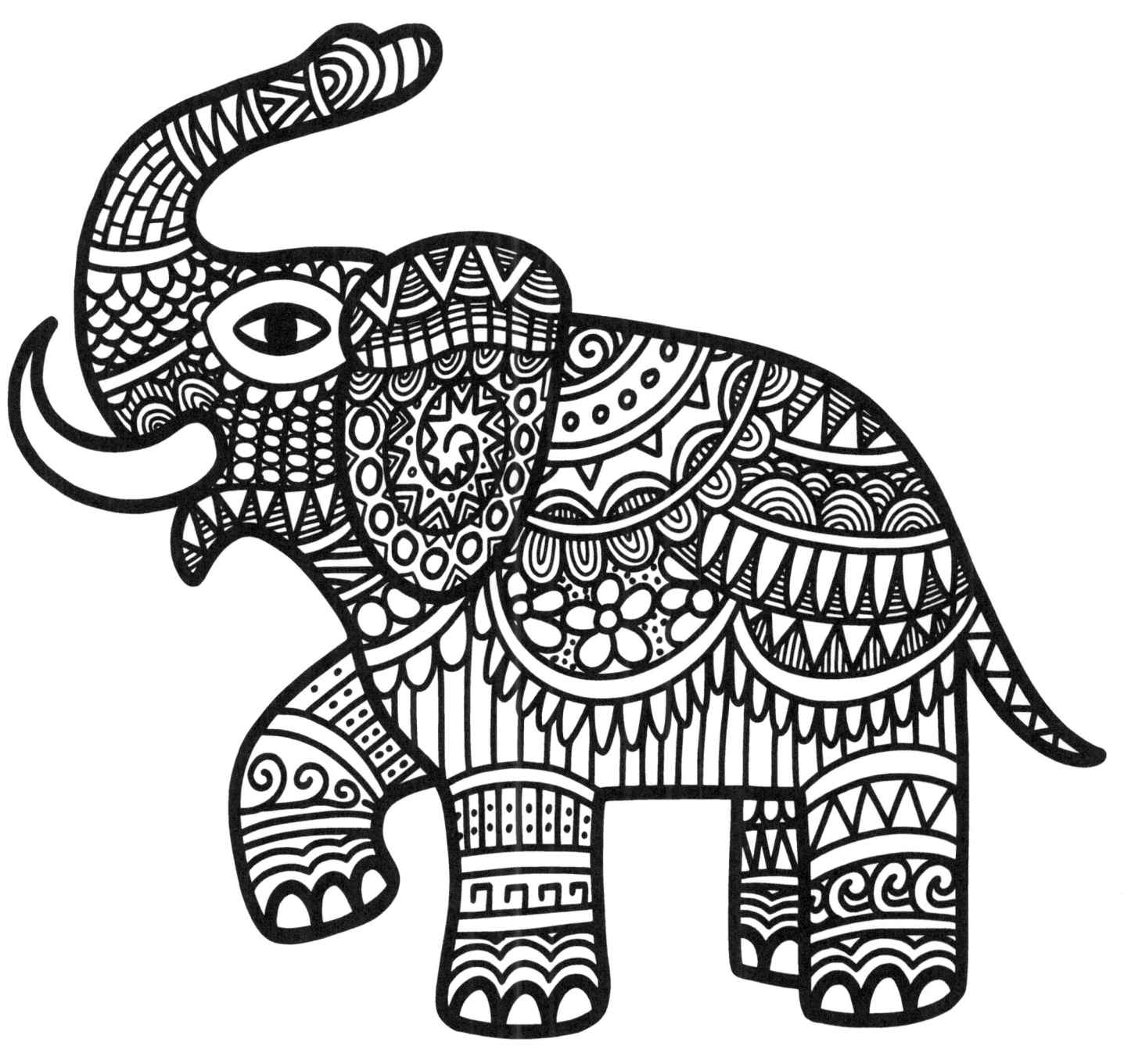

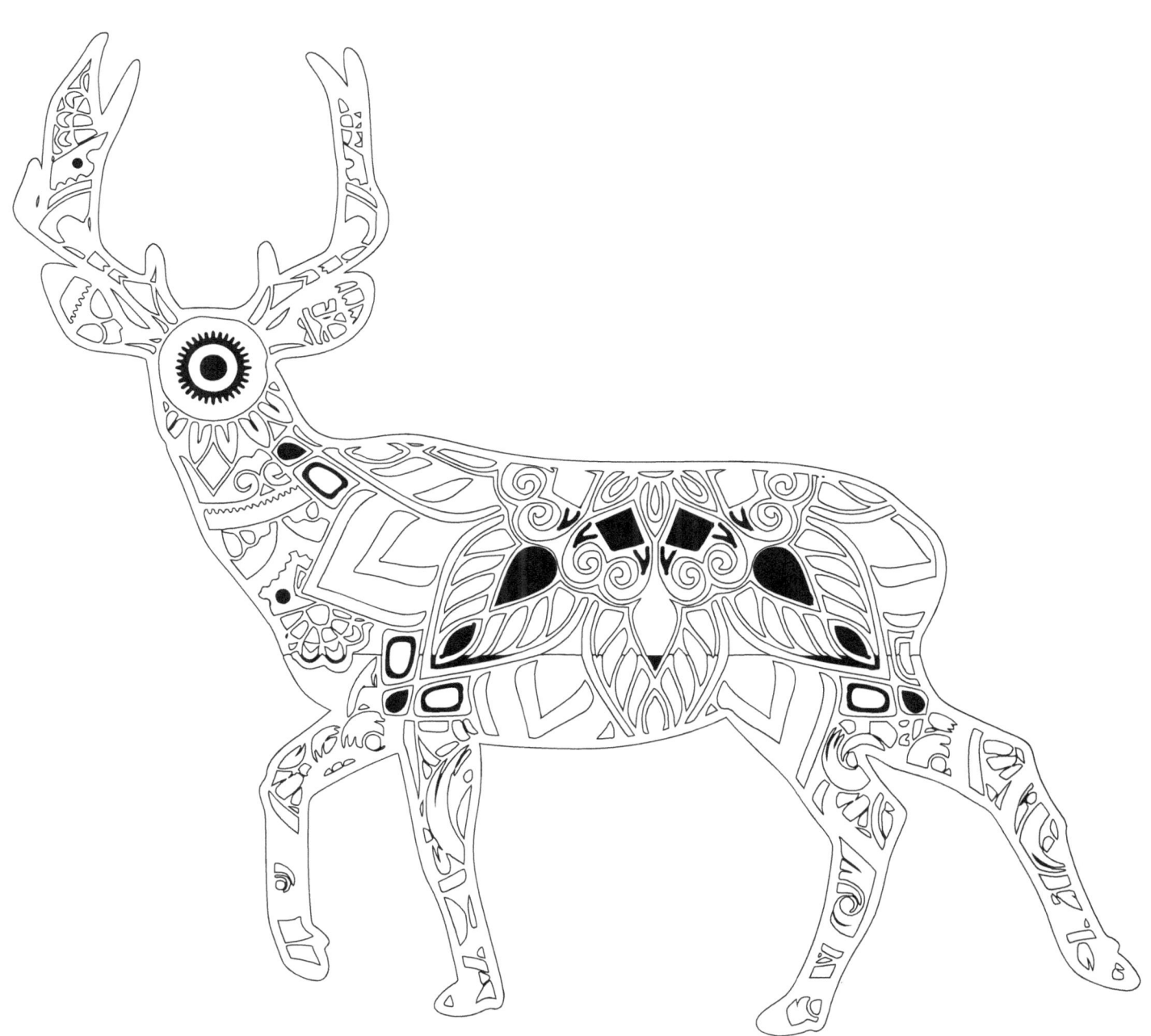

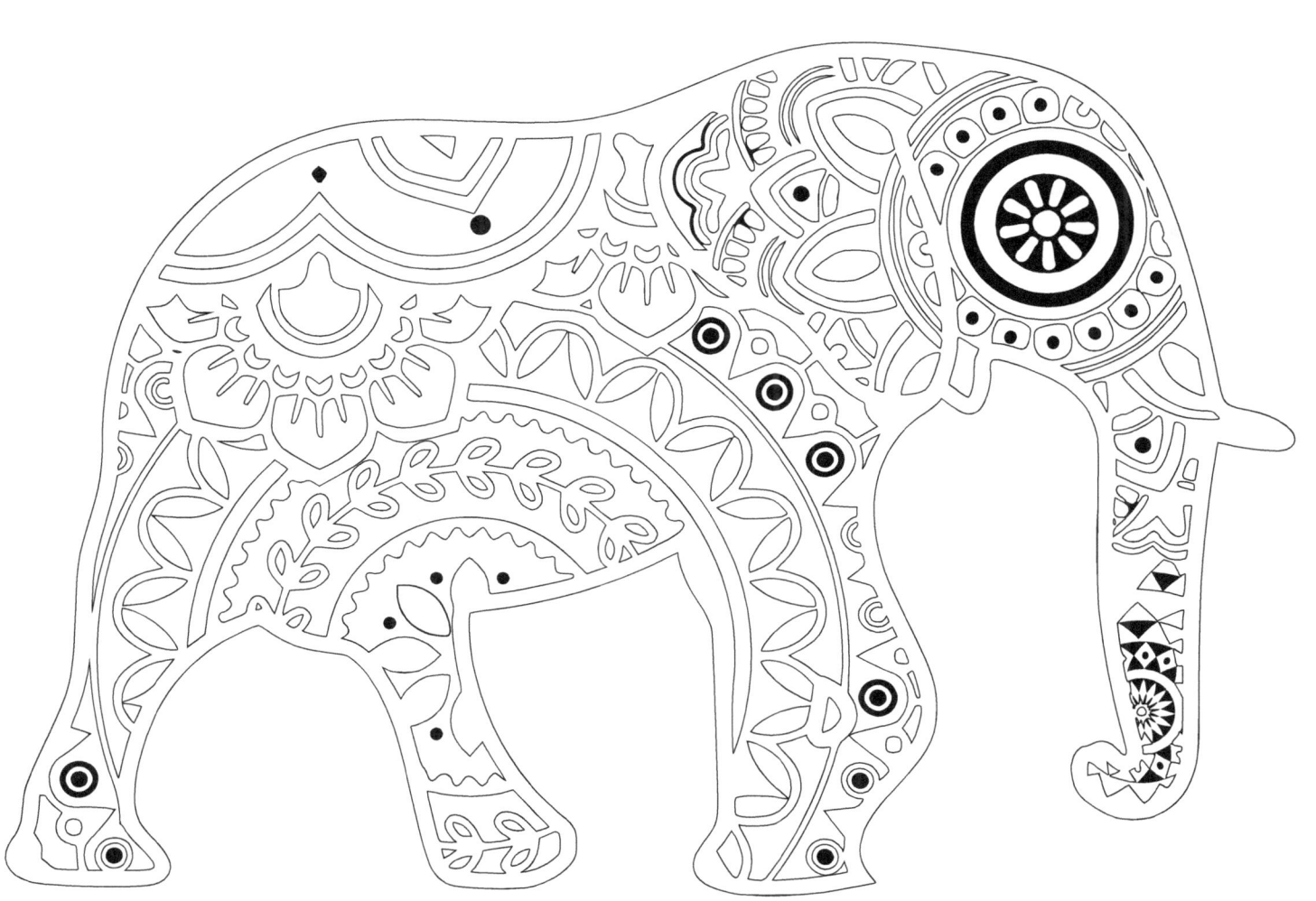

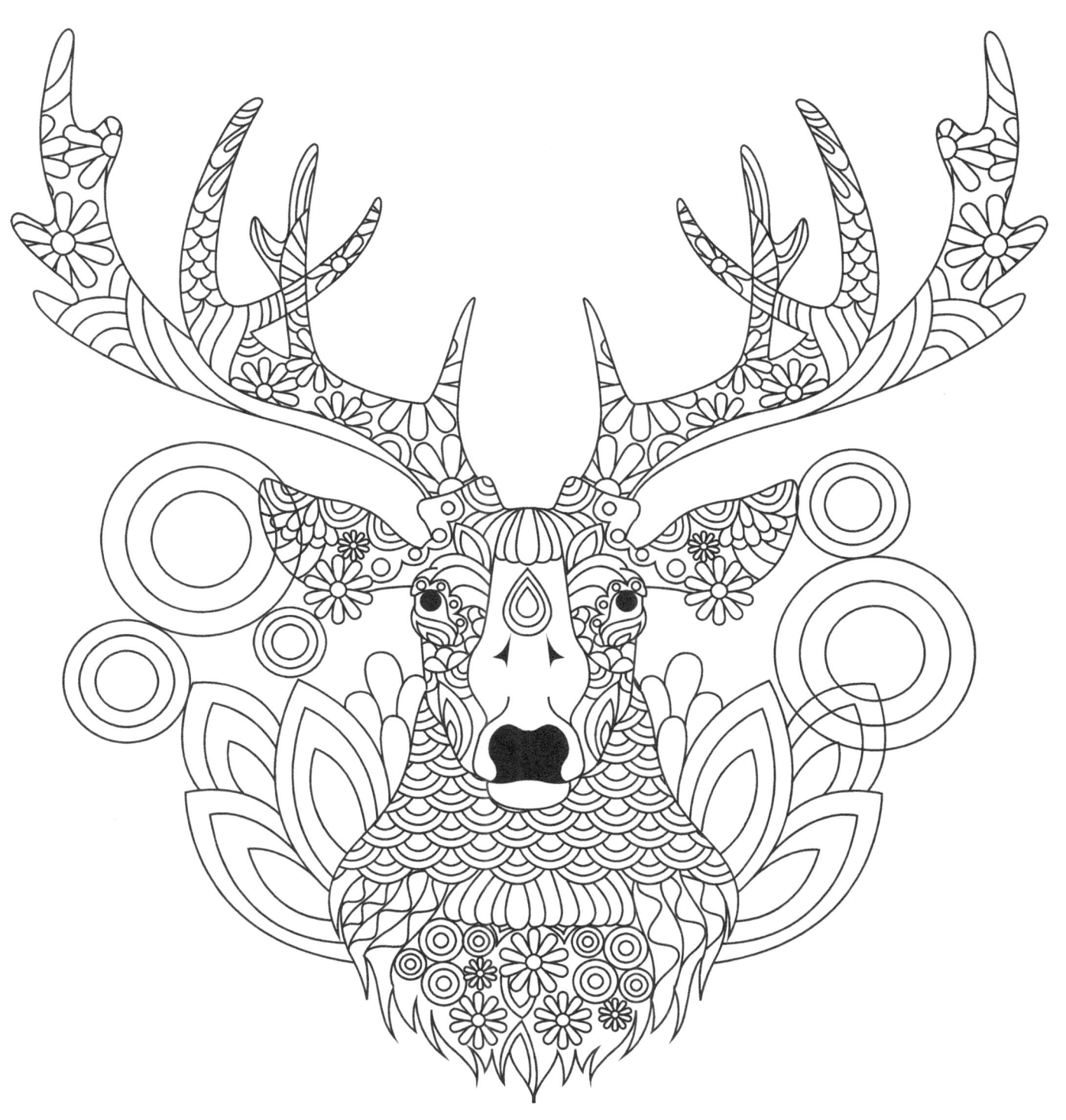

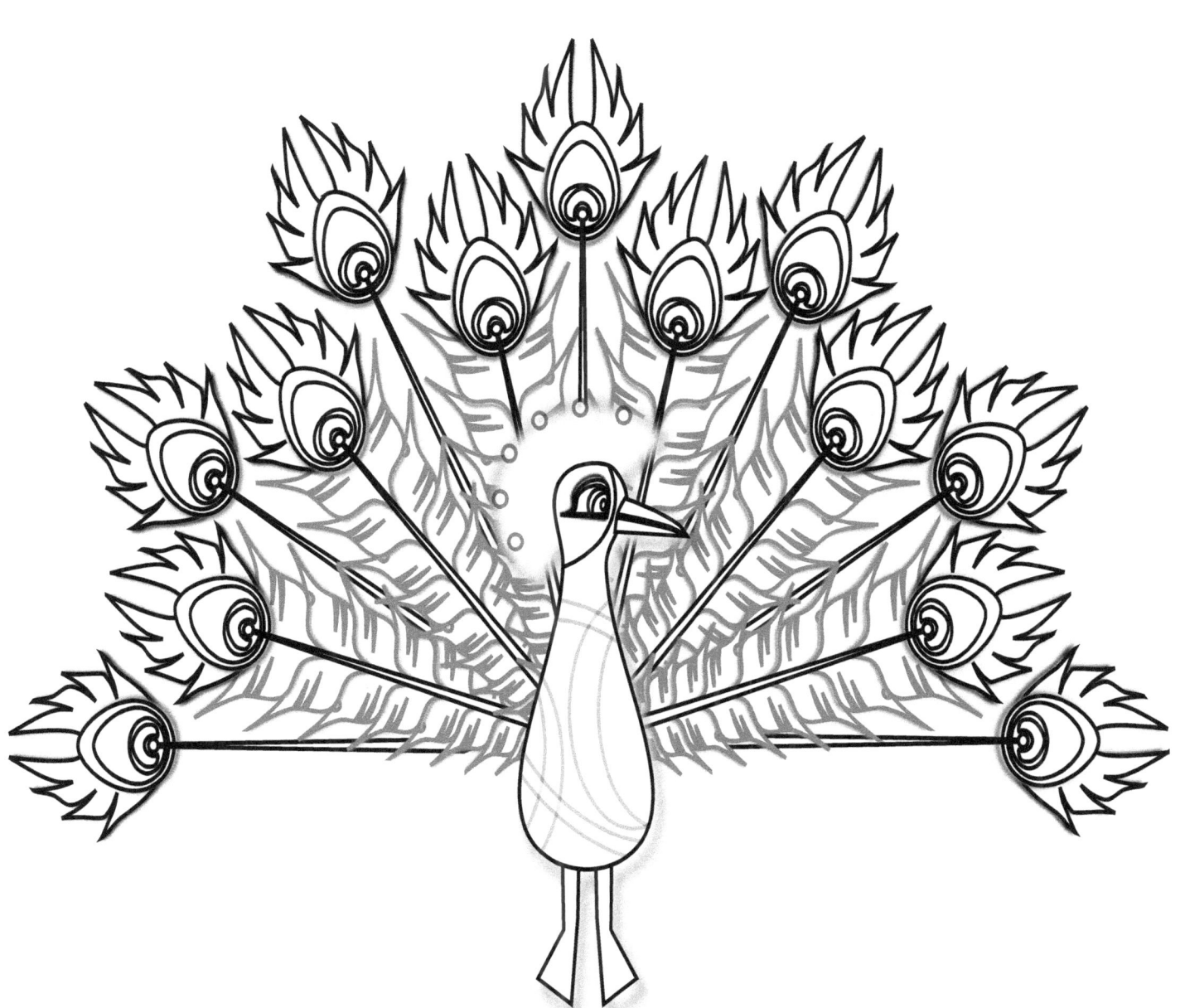